HARRY THE POLIS
AH CANNAE TELL A LIE!

. . .

HARRY MORRIS

BLACK & WHITE PUBLISHING

First published 2008
by Black & White Publishing Ltd
29 Ocean Drive, Edinburgh, EH6 6JL

1 3 5 7 9 10 8 6 4 2   08 09 10 11 12

ISBN 13   978 1 84502 232 7

Typeset by RefineCatch Ltd, Bungay, Suffolk
Printed by Norhaven A/S Denmark

• • •

This book is dedicated to
Mr Ian MacKenzie (Consultant/General Surgeon)
and all those involved in the cure for cancer.
With special thanks to the Breast Cancer Care
Nurses at Monklands Hospital, Elaine Ferguson,
Mary McGlade and Jackie O'Donnell.

• • •

Also available from Harry the Polis:

For *Absent Friends*

· · ·

'We say that the hour of death cannot be forecast, but when we say this, we imagine that hour as placed in a obscure and distant future.
It never occurs to us that it has any connection with the day already begun, or that death could arrive this same afternoon, this afternoon which is so certain and which has every hour filled in advance.'

Marcel Proust

Adopted by the charity
'The Care of Police Survivors'

Contents

• • •

Introduction

• • •

It's that time again and so, as if by pure magic, or bad luck, whichever way you want to look at it, Volume 6 in the highly successful and popular *Harry the Polis* series of books appears – 'Just like that!'

Yet another collection of stories, jokes, anecdotes and tales (and many more lies) that are intended to tempt your laughter lines to make an appearance and have you flashing your gnashers.

As per usual, like the others in the *Harry the Polis* series, you can open up this book, flick your way through it, stop anywhere you want, from beginning to end, and be certain to come across a story that will cheer you up.

It is my hope that you'll read them over and over, relating a certain joke, story or anecdote that gave you a right good laugh, or made you chuckle out loud.

You will find as you read through this book that you just can't keep some of the stories to yourself and you'll want to share them with your friends. Well go ahead.

Laughter is the best medicine, so grab a good dose of it and you'll hopefully feel much better.

Well!

What are you waiting for now?

Turn the first page and get crackin.

Harry

The Writer

· · ·

A writer died a very sudden death and arrived outside the Pearly Gates.

Within minutes of his arrival Saint Peter came out to greet him and offered him two choices:

'You can go to Hell, or you can go to Heaven!'

The writer asked Saint Peter if he would allow him a sneak preview of each place, in order to see what would be in store for him.

Saint Peter agreed to his request and escorted the writer down to Hell, where there were rows and rows of writers chained by the ankles to their desks, being whipped by demons as they typed away furiously in a flaming, steaming dungeon atmosphere.

'I don't fancy this place very much!' the writer said.

'Okay!' Saint Peter said. 'Come with me then.'

At that, Saint Peter whisked him away to Heaven, where the writer was astonished to see that nothing here was different from Hell.

Rows and rows of writers were chained to their desks, typing away, whilst also being whipped in a flaming, steaming dungeon atmosphere.

'Holy shit!' the writer remarked. 'This place is just as bad as down below in Hell!'

To which Saint Peter replied, 'No it is not . . . Up here you get published!'

This One's For You!

...

'This One's For You' is a story about my old mate Donnie Henderson, who is becoming a bit of a cult figure with the readers of *Harry the Polis* books, so I thought I'd start with him.

Donnie received a call to attend the scene of a serious road accident in Great Western Road in Glasgow.

When he arrived at the location of the accident, it was pure carnage, with body parts and bits of vehicles scattered everywhere.

Quickly, he took out his notebook and began taking notes of what he could see, a description of everything, and where it was positioned.

After writing down several pages of items, Donnie came across an accident victim's decapitated head and wrote in his notebook: 'Head on boolevard!'

This spelling didn't look right to him, so he scored it out and wrote over it.

'Head on bullavard!'

This second attempt at spelling didn't look right either, so he tried again for a third time.

'Head on boullavard!'

This spelling still didn't look right to Donnie, who was a perfectionist when submitting a report, so he looked about to make sure no one was watching him, walked over and kicked the head about five metres away, then wrote in his notebook.

'Head in nearby garden!'

You're a sick man, Donnie Henderson.

The Police Chase

...

A Glasgow senior citizen was driving his brand new Mercedes SLK 200 convertible out of his driveway for the first time, taking it on its maiden drive along the motorway.

As he drove onto the outside lane he floored it to 90 mph, thoroughly loving the wind blowing through what little hair he had left on his head.

'This is awesome!' he thought to himself, as he flew along the M8 motorway, enjoying the thrill of pushing the pedal to the metal even more.

However, when he looked in his rear-view mirror, lo and behold, there was a police car following him, with blue lights flashing and siren blaring.

Believing he was the next Lewis Hamilton, he thought to himself, 'No problem! I can outrun them and get away!' He then floored the pedal, accelerating faster. 100 mph. 110 mph. 120 mph. 130 mph.

Suddenly he thought to himself, 'What in hell's name am I doing here? I'm far too old for this reckless behaviour!' At that, he pulled over onto the hard shoulder and waited for the pursuing police car to catch him up.

As the police car pulled up behind him, an officer got out and walked up to the driver's side of the Mercedes, looked at his watch and said, 'Sir! My shift ends in exactly fifteen minutes. Today is Friday and I'm heading off for a relaxing weekend with my girlfriend. If you can provide me with a reasonable explanation as to why you were driving at speeds in excess of one hundred miles per hour, and it is an excuse that I have never heard before, then I'll let you off!'

The elderly driver looked seriously at the police officer for several moments before he replied.

'It's like this officer. Several years ago, my wife ran off with a policeman, and for one horrible moment there, I thought it was you bringing her back!'

The policeman stared at the elderly driver with a blank expression on his face and said, 'You have a good day sir!'

Nothing but the Truth
• • •

Ninety-nine per cent of today's solicitors give the rest a bad name! Allegedly.

Apparently, you're not drunk if you can lie on the floor without holding on!

And the latest survey shows that three out of four people make up seventy-five per cent of the population! According to a new poll.

Mistaken Identity

• • •

It was a quiet night with not a lot happening and my old mate Ian Taylor, the 'beat' cop for the Roystonhill area of Glasgow, was sitting in the police box, filling out his notebook, when suddenly he was disturbed by the sound of heavy footsteps approaching in his direction.

On opening the door to the police box, he saw what appeared to be his police colleague chasing after a ned-type person, up the hill towards his position.

Ian immediately sprang into action, drew his police truncheon and – WALLOP!

He struck the ned, who promptly dropped to the ground like a sack of potatoes. At that, Ian jumped on top of him and whilst holding the struggling ned down, he proceeded to berate him for running away from the police, whilst administering a further couple of WALLOPS in order to enforce his authority.

At that moment, a rather puffed-out and knackered police colleague arrived at the scene and managed to blurt out, 'For fuxsakes, Ian, get aff him, he's just been informed his wife is having a baby, right now! As we speak! So we were both heading for his house to try and lend a hand until the ambulance arrived!'

As Ian released his grip, the expectant father, now slightly groggy and worse for wear, set off again, pursued this time by two very unfit, breathless polis, who arrived in time to see the ambulance leaving the house with expectant mother on board.

They never found out whether the baby was a boy or

girl, but you can be sure its father had a right good bedtime story to tell, when it was older!

Rabbit! Rabbit! Rabbit!
• • •

One evening whilst on desk duty in the police station, the door opened and in walked a very irate male carrying a squashed dead rabbit.

He dropped it onto my office desk and said in an aggressive voice, 'Some bastard dumped this dead rabbit at my front door and I've just found it when I arrived home from work!'

I looked at his face full of anger, as he stared back at me with steam coming out of his ears.

'So you want to report that you've just found it?' I said.

'Too right I want to report it!' he replied.

To which I couldn't resist saying, 'Okay, sir! Give me your full name and address, and if nobody claims it within three months, you can keep it!'

Not exactly the response he was looking for, but it did eventually get through to him and provoke a laugh!

The Braehead Scam

...

This is a 'News Flash' for you and any of your friends who may be regular customers at Braehead Shopping Centre.

I hate to admit it, but over the last month, I have become the victim of a very clever scam whilst out shopping.

Simply going out to buy some bits and pieces has turned out to be quite a traumatic experience for me, and don't you dare be so naïve to think it couldn't happen to you.

Here's how the scam works:

Two seriously good-looking young girls of about 19 or 20 years old come over to your car as you are loading your bags of messages into your boot.

They both begin cleaning your windscreen with a cloth and some Windolene, exposing their cleavage, and with their neatly refined breasts almost falling out of their skimpy wet T-shirts. It is impossible not to notice, or afford oneself a second look.

When you thank them and offer to pay, they bluntly refuse any payment, but instead ask you for a lift to Clydebank.

Unable to resist their request, you agree, and they both climb into the back seat of your car.

On the way to Clydebank, they start kissing and caressing each other, and before you can say stop, they're having lesbian sex in the back of your car.

Moments later, one of them climbs over into the front seat of the car and begins to perform a sexual act on you, as you drive along the road. While this is happening, the other one slips her hand into your jacket pocket and relieves you of your wallet.

As a result of this act, I've had my wallet stolen on November 4th, 9th, 10th, twice on the 12th, 18th, 21st, and three times yesterday. And just for the record, it's a certainty to happen again this weekend, just as soon as I can buy some more wallets!

Harry's Police Contacts Page

· · ·

Former Grampian police officer, recently retired, 52 years old, widowed, not exactly Robert Redford in the looks department but have a new car, my own house and a right good pension, in desperate need of a right good ride. Anything considered.
Police Box 17/01.

Kiss it Better!

...

Several years ago, all police officers were trained in the use of the new side-handled baton, or PR24, to give it the proper name.

I was never any good at using it and preferred to use my patter to get me out of trouble, rather than my baton.

One particular evening, I was accompanied by a young female officer, who shall remain anonymous, when we received a call to attend a complaint regarding a stray dog causing annoyance at someone's house in the Port Glasgow area.

As we arrived at the address and got out of the police panda car, I saw a placid-looking dog in the front garden of the house, and it greeted us by wagging its tail. It didn't bother us, or do anything to suggest this was the dog referred to in the complaint, so as we approached and entered the front door, the dog followed us inside.

As a result of this action by the dog, I naturally assumed it belonged to the householder.

'What's the problem?' I asked the woman of the house.

'That is,' she replied, pointing to the dog that had followed us inside. 'It's not mine, and whenever anyone comes to my door, it won't let them leave the garden!'

Trapped in her house, I sarcastically thanked her for informing the police control of the precise problem.

As we attempted to leave and return to our police vehicle, the once placid-looking dog bared his teeth, snarled and growled at our slightest movement.

Earlier in my police service I had the unfortunate

distinction of having been attacked by an Alsatian dog and was not about to allow this to happen a second time. So I pushed the young policewoman in front of me for protection . . .

No I didn't, I'm only joking, but it did cross my mind!

I quickly came to the decision that this was an occasion where I might just be required to use my PR24 police baton.

Drawing it from my holster I flicked it outwards in order to extend it fully, and remembering my training, I swung it around at waist height in an attempt to smack the dog on the nose.

This was apparently a tried and tested method of chasing off neds, so therefore it was sure to have the same response with an aggressive dog!

However, in the adrenalin-filled excitement of trying to fend off the dog, I completely missed my target and unfortunately struck my young female colleague, who was standing behind me, waist high!

She immediately let out a scream of pain and doubled over.

My response was to look at her and say, 'For Christ's sake, stand up and try and look professional. People are watching you!'

In all the confusion taking place, the dog received such a fright that it ran like the clappers along the road. Obviously it was thinking to itself, 'If he does that to his colleague, what might he do to me?'

We made it back to the police vehicle, where I checked if she was alright, to which she whimpered and moaned.

I apologised for the entire episode and volunteered to kiss her tummy better, trying to humour her.

'You didn't hit my tummy! You're not that good at aiming!' she replied in a slightly deeper voice.

As a result of my wild swing at the dog, I had actually struck her downstairs in the ladies' department.

Totally embarrassed by this, my face turned bright red, but I couldn't resist reiterating my initial offer to kiss it better, should she feel the urge to take it up!

From that day onwards, my PR24 police baton remained in its holster. Mind you, this was the second time that disaster had struck, having previously in my probation inadvertently clobbered a former colleague with my old-fashioned wooden baton, breaking his wrist and his LCD 'Kojak' watch. Purely by accident, of course.

Honest!

God Bless Us All

• • •

The policeman on duty outside the entrance to the House of Commons once asked the House Chaplain if he ever prayed for the members.

The Chaplain replied with a straight face. 'No! I usually take one look at them and pray for the country!'

Polis on a Horse

...

A mounted police officer patrolling on his horse had occasion to stop a little girl while she was riding along the road on her bicycle.

He asked her, 'Did you get that bike for your Christmas, from Santa Claus?'

'Yes!' the little girl replied, pleased with herself.

'Well!' the police officer said. 'The next time you write him a letter, you inform Santa that you require to have fitted to your bike a red reflective light at the rear and a white light to the front of it!'

At that, he fined her for committing the offence and issued her with a £5 ticket.

The little girl took possession of the ticket, then looked up at the mounted police officer and said, 'That's a nice horse you have there, Officer, did Santa Claus bring you that for your Christmas?'

The police officer chuckled and replied, 'He sure did, sweetheart.'

At which point the little girl responded, 'Well the next time you write him a letter, you tell Santa that the dick goes under the horse, not on top of it!'

Bridget's Date

· · ·

When Bridget the policewoman was a teenager she contracted a disease of the gums and had to have all her teeth extracted by the dentist and false teeth fitted.

This particular evening she had been to the dancing and her date asked her on the way home if she would like a bag of chips, to which she replied, 'Yesh!'

As they sat at the rear of the bus with their chips, munching away, Bridget suddenly sneezed. As a result of this her newly fitted false teeth came flying out of her mouth, landing in his chip poke.

Her date immediately burst out laughing at this, and seeing the funny side of it herself, Bridget laughed as well. In fact she laughed so much and so hard that she couldn't stop herself from farting out loud. This unexpected burst of flatulence coincided with a huge snotter bubble appearing out of her nose.

The two love birds laughed uncontrollably at the rear of the bus, him with Bridget's false teeth decorating his chip poke and her with snotters and tears blinding her from laughing so loud, all accompanied by the intermittent sound of flatulence being passed.

But after that memorable night, she never heard from him again.

I wonder why, Bridget? Maybe some guys just have no taste!

A Rouble Millionaire

· · ·

After an exhausting, energy-sapping concert, all we wanted to do in the band was head back to our hotel room and crash out on the bed – with a large whisky in one's hand, I might add!

However, we had performed live on Russian TV earlier on that afternoon and the producer of the programme and well-known celebrity and quiz show host from Moscow, Dimitri Deeprov, had invited us all out for a meal after our concert that evening.

On arriving back at the hotel, we quickly unloaded all of our equipment and instruments and changed out of our concert clothes of tartan kilts and sark shirts.

Dimitri arrived right on time and joined some of us in my room for a few large glasses of Black Bottle whisky, prior to heading out.

As we prepared to leave the hotel, Dimitri said we should bring the whisky with us, as it was only a short walk to the restaurant and we could finish it on the way.

Now, in Moscow, it is not an offence to drink on the street, so being greedy whisky drinkers, we took advantage of their laws, and brought along an extra bottle to down on the way!

As we reached the restaurant, we stood outside for a few moments while we emptied our bottles of the remaining amber liquid, then entered the restaurant and were shown immediately to our table, which had been reserved by Dimitri.

Several diners came over and asked Dimitri for his autograph and, while signing for them, he introduced us. Not being clad in our costume gear of tartan kilts, etc, we were not instantly recognisable at that time, although we were getting plenty of exposure for our visit from the newspapers and TV station.

We settled down and the waiter appeared with what looked like two jugs of water in fancy crystal decanters, but turned out to be their very own brand of 45% vodka, straight from the freezer.

'A toast!' Dimitri said, getting to his feet, while the waiters topped up our small shot glasses with this aircraft fuel.

There was a pause while we waited for the restaurant owner and a photographer to join us at our table.

Glasses in hand and up to the mouth. 'Nostrovia!' from the host and 'Slainte!' from us as we all in unison downed our glasses.

At this point I might add that drinking shots of 45% vodka, with no label to describe it, on top of all that Black Bottle whisky, might just seem like a good idea at the particular moment, but it was not the most refreshing thing I've ever drunk, that's for sure!

Now the custom is, you continue downing the vodka until your food arrives, but unfortunately for us, this wasn't a fast-food venue!

By the time the food was being served, I had made two visits to other diners' tables to retrieve and restrain Angus, who had climbed up on top of one table and was attempting to demonstrate some kind of Highland Fling, while dancing between their cutlery.

Every one of us was now ravenous and prepared to eat the waiter if he didn't hurry up and place the food on the table.

We were like a pack of wild dogs as we wolfed the food down. I didn't know what I was eating, but under the influence and having consumed so much alcohol, I didn't really care what it was.

'Would you like asparagus?' the waiter asked, referring to the soup.

'No thanks, I don't eat sparrows and, please, don't call me Gus!' quipped Angus, who then asked the waiter to bring him chopsticks and had to be reminded that we were in Russia, not China. So because he couldn't get chopsticks, he used his fingers to eat his food, and ended up wearing most of it on his face and shirt.

It was time for Angus to bid farewell to the rest of the diners and head for his kennel – sorry, hotel room.

He could hardly stand on his own two feet, as the alcohol had now totally overcome him.

I helped him up, made excuses for him and, with my arm under his shoulder, holding him up, I left the restaurant for the comfort and safety of the hotel room.

As we walked the short journey back to the hotel, Angus became heavier and heavier as his legs appeared to give up performing any natural function of their own.

We continued to sway from side to side, narrowly avoiding the high drop from the pavement onto the busy five-lane road.

At last, the doors of the Marriott Hotel were in sight, however, unfortunately for us, so was a big Russian polis, who was standing between us and the door entrance, clad in his impressive police uniform and jack boots with a Kalashnikov machine gun hanging from a shoulder strap.

Just beyond him, sitting in their patrol car was his partner, looking out at us.

'Angus! Angus! Get a grip of yourself and try and act normal, there's a big polis with a gun blocking our path to the door of the hotel, so let me do the talking!'

As I went to negotiate my way around him, carrying Angus, he put his hand across my chest, stopped us and began shouting at me in Russian.

Despite having just drunk half of Moscow's vodka supply, it still didn't help me to understand him, or for me to be able to converse in Russian, so I tried to explain.

'We are Scotlandia, we stay in this hotel!' I shouted back.

That said, I tried to walk past him to the hotel entrance.

He quickly put his arm across my chest like before, only with much more force, and started shouting again.

So I tried explaining again.

'We are Scotlandia, we stay in this hotel, here, comrade!'

Again he put his hand across my chest, blocking me.

I pulled Angus up and said, 'Well, son, I think we're getting the jail, so keep cool and say nothing!'

No sooner had I said these words, when Angus tried to put his arm around the policeman's neck and said, 'Och gie's a cuddle ya big hunk!'

He immediately pushed Angus's arm away, stepped back and pointed his gun at us, as his partner got out from the police car.

'Woah! Woah! Cool the beans, big man, we're only two drunken Scotsmen, we're no' exactly terrorists,' I responded, gripping hold of Angus and holding him up.

Fortunately, Dimitri and the others saw what was happening, had caught up with us and were there in minutes.

Dimitri intervened and was instantly recognised by the policemen.

He spoke with them for a moment then whispered out of the side of his mouth to me.

'Go, Harry, go now with Angus!'

Now, having sobered up rapidly, I carried out Dimitri's instructions to a tee and practically burst through the hotel door, tripping and falling over on top of Angus, whereby he sustained heavy swelling and a perfect black eye for his troubles.

Shortly after this, we were joined inside by Dimitri, who appeared to find the entire episode extremely funny.

He explained that you while can drink on the streets of Moscow, you can't appear drunk or stagger about, otherwise you encounter the situation that we just did, and you get the jail.

How did Dimitri get us off? Simple: he hosts the Russian version of *Who Wants to be a Millionaire?* and supplied them with tickets for the show.

By the way, unlike in the UK where the winning contestant receives a million pounds sterling, in Russia you get a million roubles, which works out to be about £200!

Not exactly a fortune there, I can assure you.

Finally, the following day, our Russian tour agent called

at the hotel and I informed him about the incident, and the fact that they were going to arrest us.

'Not at all, Harry. They might have taken you to the station, but as soon as they found out who you both were, they would have released you both after five minutes. Trust me!' he said.

'Five minutes?' I thought to myself. 'That sounds like just long enough to be sexually abused by the entire station!'

Somehow, his reassurances didn't sound too convincing to me!

Sophie's Choice

...

A man woke up in the hospital today, to discover he was swathed in bandages from head to foot.

The doctor, doing his rounds came in to see him and said, 'Ah, I see you have regained consciousness. Now, you probably don't remember anything, but you were involved in a car pile-up on the motorway. You're going to be okay, you'll walk again and everything, but . . . well, I'm sorry to have to tell you this, and I'm trying to break it to you gently, but the fact is your penis was chopped off in the accident, and the emergency services in attendance were unable to find it anywhere!'

The man was very upset by this tragic news and began to moan and groan, but the doctor continued.

'However, the good news is you have £10,000 of insurance compensation coming to you and we now have the technology to build you a brand new penis that will perform as good as your old one did – in fact, probably even better! The only thing is, it doesn't come cheap. It works out at £1,000 per inch!'

The man stopped groaning and perked up at this news.

'So!' the doctor said. 'It's for you to decide just how many inches you would like. But maybe it's a decision you'd better discuss with your wife. I mean, if you had a five-inch penis before the accident, you might decide to go for double that, although she might be a bit put out. On the other hand, if you were well endowed before and had a ten-inch one, and you decide to invest in only a five-incher this time, she might be considerably disappointed.

Therefore, as I said, it's important that she play a role in helping you make the right decision.'

The man agreed to talk it over with his wife.

The following day the doctor returned to hear his decision.

'So, did you talk it over with your wife?' he asked.

'I did,' the man replied.

'And did she help you to come to a decision?'

'She has,' the man said.

'So, what is it going to be? Five or ten inches?' the doctor asked.

To which the man replied rather dejectedly, 'Neither! Sophie's decided . . . we're getting a new kitchen!'

Was That Sore?

· · ·

A police officer became the unlikely and unexpected victim of assault whilst on uniform duty at a flower festival.

It appears that while he was in attendance, delivering to the members of the public the various methods of personal safety, security and advice on garden shed alarms, an elderly lady approached him and jokingly asked if she could view his PR24 police-issue baton.

The usual good-hearted banter and laughter spread among those present, particularly when the elderly lady gently tapped him on the arm.

More laughter ensued as the police officer feigned injury at her blow.

Still giggling like a young schoolgirl and without the slightest warning of what was to come next, she took a full swing with the baton and struck the officer a WALLOP on his head, just as he was getting up from the floor.

His knees buckled from the blow and he had to be assisted.

As for the elderly lady, she almost collapsed with shock, having realised she had delivered such a hefty blow.

All became clear later, when she explained that she thought his police cap was made of a tougher material, like a helmet!

Oh, how times change. It used to be they asked to be handcuffed . . .

Now you're talking!

Mental Hospital Phone Menu

・・・

Hello and thank you for calling the State Mental Hospital. Please select from the following options:

If you have an obsessive-compulsive illness, press 1 repeatedly.

If you are co-dependent, please ask someone nearby to press 2 for you.

If you have multiple personalities, press 3, 4, 5 and 6.

If you are paranoid, we know who you are and what you want, so stay on the line so we can trace your call.

If you are delusional, press 7 and your call will be forwarded to the Mother Ship.

If you are schizophrenic, listen very carefully, and a little voice will tell which number(s) to press.

If you are manic-depressive, it doesn't matter which number you press, nothing will make you happy anyway.

If you are dyslexic, press 96969696969696.

If you are bi-polar, please leave a message after the beep, or before the beep, or after the beep. Please wait for the beep.

If you have short-term memory loss, press 9. If you have short-term memory loss, press 9. If you have short-term memory loss, press 9.

If you have low self-esteem, please hang up. Our operators are far too busy to talk with you.

If you are menopausal, please put the gun down! Hang up, turn on the fan, lie down and cry. It only lasts for a short period.

If you are blonde, don't press any buttons, you'll just mess up.

This coming week is National Mental Health Care Week. You can do your part by remembering to contact at least one unstable person to show you care.
(Well, my job is done. Now it's your turn!)

The Blonde Story
. . .

A blonde woman returns home to discover her house has been broken into.

Upset by this discovery, she immediately contacts the police to report it and demands that they send over a patrol car to deal with it right away.

The police controller informs her that the only patrol car nearest to her home is a canine car.

The hysterical blonde screams at the controller that she doesn't care what it is – 'Just send the bloody thing over!'

Moments later, a police vehicle screeches to a stop outside her house.

The blonde woman looks out of her window and sees a policeman getting out the vehicle, holding onto his Alsatian dog.

She squeals out loud, 'Just my fucking luck! My house gets robbed and they send over a blind policeman!'

Arthur or Martha?

· · ·

A man I had great admiration for during the best part of my police service at Glasgow Sheriff Court in the seventies was the renowned Sheriff J. Irvine Smith, who was feared by the neds as being a 'heavy hitter'.

In other words, he handed out proper monetary and custodial sentences to fit the crimes being committed.

He was also widely acknowledged and credited with being the Sheriff whom, after hearing an accused give his lame excuse as to why he had failed to appear at court on the correct date and time, listened intently to him before responding with the famous line:

'Do you honestly think I came up the Clyde in a banana boat?'

There was also the time when a young transvestite appeared before him, still sprightly dressed up and looking the part as an attractive young female.

It was alleged that after hearing the case against the accused, the Sheriff deferred sentence for several weeks, instructing him to go home, maintain a low profile and steer clear of any other trouble, by basically behaving like a good little girl until the next court appearance!

No one had the nerve to tell him that's why he/she was appearing before him in the first place.

A-ttention!

. . .

Alistair was of the old school in the City of Glasgow police, and, being ex-army, he was always immaculately turned out, with iron creases on his shirts and trousers so sharp that they could take the 7 o'clock shadow clean off your face with one swipe! Coupled with his boots that were so highly bulled up you could see your face in them.

All the above was complemented by his pencil-thin Clark Gable moustache and a hairstyle in vogue at the moment: that of the completely bald shiny napper!

Alistair's beat consisted of the now defunct Kingston Docks with its huge sheds and it was considered amongst many of the shift as a punishment detail to work there. However, it was a detail that didn't faze Alistair, who went about his duties on his own with only the pigeons for company. Some even suggested he was on first-name terms with them all!

One night, while attending a call at the rear of the docks, John Thompson and Dick Bruce decided that whilst there, they would pay Alistair a visit and have a blether.

After several minutes, driving around the area, they came across a shed with the door slightly open, and as they stopped outside it, they could hear shouting.

As they both entered the shed, being ex-army, they both recognised that the shouting was actually someone calling out military drill commands. 'Lefffftt turn! By the lefffftt quick march! Left, right, left, right, left . . .Company . . . Halt!'

Intrigued by what they were hearing, they both looked down the bottom of the shed, where they observed Alistair, his police baton under his right arm, smartly marching back and forwards, calling out the precise orders and executing every drill movement with perfection. It was a sight that any Regimental Sergeant Major would have been proud of.

After several minutes of watching Alistair, they decided to leave him to his drill movements, although John swears that Dick was getting itchy feet and was beginning to carry out some of the commands on the spot!

They later learned that this behaviour was normal for Alistair at that time of night, in the sheds of the derelict dock area, with no one to talk to except for the pigeons. Co-Coo! Coo! Coo!

That's pigeon English for 'Company Halt! Halt! Halt!'

Harry's Moneysaving Ideas
• • •

Don't spend any more money getting your shirts laundered.

What you do is hand the dirty ones into your local charity shop, and after they've washed and ironed them, you buy them back! They're definitely much cheaper than the prices charged at the laundrette!

National Service

· · ·

When National Service was in force in Britain, a young man who received the call to attend pleaded he had a very bad eyesight problem.

He was given all the usual tests and, sure enough, he failed them all.

In desperation, the medical examiner held up a car tyre and asked, 'Can you describe to me what I am holding up?'

The young man blinked several times before answering, 'It's either a two-shilling coin, or half a crown!'

Due to his failure to recognise it was a tyre, he was not accepted for National Service.

As a result of this rejection on medical grounds, he went out to celebrate his good fortune, deciding to treat himself with a visit to the cinema.

He took his seat and hadn't been there long when, to his horror, who should take the seat beside him but the medical examiner, who instantly recognised him.

Quick as a flash, the rejected conscript said, 'Is this the right bus for Govan?'

Which reminds me of the time when I was in the Royal Engineers and, on parade, the Sergeant Major asked, 'Are any of you lot here particularly fond of music?'

Immediately, several of the Channel Islanders and Welsh lads threw their hands up with gusto.

To which he responded, 'Right, fall out and report to the canteen and shift the piano!'

Toe Nails?

• • •

Having recently returned from picket line duty at the Lady Victoria Colliery during the miners' strike, and still sporting the bruises to prove it, Dick was back out on his beat patrol in the Woodburn housing scheme at Dalkeith, affectionately referred to by the locals as The Bronx.

It was a quiet Sunday and he was just enjoying the peace of an early morning, when all was shattered by a woman appearing in the street in front of him, screaming and squealing hysterically as she ran towards him.

He instantly recognised her as the loudmouth trouble maker of the area, 'Sweaty' Betty McDougal, closely followed by two of her thieving sons . . . Allegedly!

'Quick! Come quick! Its ma daddy. Hurry!' she shouted.

He followed her to the house, with fingers crossed that if it was a sudden illness he had suffered, it wasn't trivial!

As he entered the midden of a house with its over-whelming stench of shit and urine, he was led into the living room area, where old man McDougal was sat in his chair in front of the fire, face contorted with pain, with both his bare feet nailed to the floor.

'What sadistic bastard did that to you?' Dick asked.

'The silly auld bugger did it tae himself,' Sweaty replied, quite matter of fact. 'An armchair demonstration, he called it! Anyways, ah was in my bed and just heard him moaning. When ah came through, he was sitting in his chair – like that!'

'Hoh, Granda! Who the hell dae ye think ye are – Jesus?' one of the grandsons asked.

'Shut yer gub! Ya insensitive wee diddy,' snapped Sweaty.

Apparently he had taken this drastic and painful action the previous night, after downing a bottle of vodka in protest at the miners' strike, and only realised the painful consequences of his actions when he awoke from his drunken sleep and tried to get up out of his chair to go to the toilet.

Now, with the alcohol rapidly wearing off, he was experiencing extreme pain – as well as bursting for a much needed pee!

'D'you want a drink o' water, Granda?' he was asked.

'Stop bloody annoying him! He's liable tae pish himsel' and ruin my chair any minute!' Sweaty blurted out.

An ambulance was summoned, and whilst awaiting its arrival, Sweaty asked the cop, 'Can ye no' dae somethin' tae relieve his pain?'

(Dick thought for a moment. 'Yeah! We could call a vet and have him put down. Now that would work! Na, too good'!)

However, in an attempt to free him and alleviate his excruciating pain, Dick picked up the claw hammer that the old man had used to carry out this horrific hammer and nail trick.

He then asked Sweaty and her sons to hold him down tightly, while he extracted the four-inch nails from his feet.

His squeals could be heard along the length of the street and beyond.

Shortly after this, the Paramedics arrived and tended to the old man before carrying him out on a stretcher to the waiting ambulance, and whisked him off to hospital, but not before they had a word with Dick with regards to his 'first-aid' action.

It would appear that the police officer should have lifted the wooden floorboards to prevent further injury and suffering being sustained by the old man.

Dick explained that it was his belief that he was acting in the best interests of the old man, and at the request of his next of kin – namely Sweaty – before politely adding that he was a police officer, not a joiner, and therefore the injuries sustained by their patient were self-inflicted prior to the involvement of the police!

This drastic action adds a new meaning to the idea of wearing false nails!

It is worth mentioning that during the coal miners' strike, several police officers sustained minor injuries at the hands of the miners, and several miners sustained major injuries at the hands of the police!

Only joking, Arfur!

That's My Mother!

• • •

'Harry! Can ye come over, I need tae see you, son!'

That was the first message on my answer machine and it was from my mother, who sounded slightly upset.

I immediately called her and she answered right away.

'It's Harry, what's up?' I asked, concerned by her message.

'Och, I'll tell you about it when you come over. I'm just a bit upset!' she replied.

'Right! I'm on my way,' I said, replacing the phone.

I picked up my house keys and ran out the front door, before I realised I had no car keys. As I ran back up the stairs, I could hear my telephone ringing, and I rushed back inside to answer it. 'Hello!' But I was too late.

I waited to hear the message, which again was from my mother.

'Is that you, Harry? Christ, you don't stay in for long. Anyways, it's your mum again. Can you bring me over a fish supper from the chippie up the road? It'll save me having to make something for my dinner.'

Having fortunately heard the message, I stopped off, bought her a fish supper, then arrived at her house, and there she was, totally engrossed in watching *River City* on the TV.

'What's the big panic? What's up?' I asked.

'Och, it's that lot down at the doctor's surgery. They called me this morning and asked me to come down. There's something wrong with my thyroid!' she said. 'Now, I don't know how that can be, 'cause I take my pills every day. They're at it! Anyways, I walked in and the nurse said they had found something and so they were prescribing stronger pills! I just told her straight that I'm fed up to the teeth wi' them. They keep finding something else wrong wi' me every bloody time I go down. I'm just fed up wi' it. I've told her, 'That's it, I'm no' coming back!'

Now excuse me, but is that not what a doctor is meant to do?

Van Graffiti

• • •

Just passed a van today that displayed a notice on the rear: 'NO HAND SIGNALS'. Driver convicted Arab shoplifter!

Then I saw another one with an official notice on the rear saying, 'HOW AM I DRIVING?' Presumably you passed a test?

What next: 'WHERE AM I GOING?' or 'PLEASE PASS QUIETLY, DRIVER ASLEEP' or 'DON'T DRINK AND DRIVE, ROLL A JOINT AND FLY HOME!'

And the best advice of all: 'IF YOUR WIFE WANTS TO LEARN TO DRIVE, FOR FUXSAKES, DON'T STAND IN HER WAY!'

Speeding

...

An elderly lady was stopped for speeding. As the police officer approached her driver window, she asked, 'Is there a problem, Officer?'

'Yes, ma'am,' the officer replied. 'You've been stopped for speeding. Can I see your driver's licence?'

'I'd love to let you see it, but I don't have one,' she replied.

'You don't have a driver's licence?' the officer asked.

'No! Unfortunately, I lost it three years ago for drink driving.'

'Well, who is the registered owner of the car?' he asked.

'I don't know, Officer,' she replied. 'I just stole it today!'

'Are you telling me this is a stolen car you're driving?'

'Yes!' she responded. 'And I'd also like to confess to killing the owner of it!'

'You what?' the startled officer replied.

'I killed the owner,' she repeated calmly. 'I've chopped up his body and stuffed it into some black plastic bin bags in the boot of the car! Do you want to see them?'

The officer was stunned by her confession and slowly backed off to his police vehicle and called for some back-up.

Within minutes, several police cars arrived at the scene, where the senior officer slowly approached the elderly woman's car, his hand tightly gripping his gun in its holster.

He ordered the driver to step out of her car.

Once outside her car she asked, 'Is there a problem here, Officer?'

'There sure is, ma'am,' he replied. 'One of my officers has just reported that you have stolen this car and murdered the owner!'

'Me!' she responded, surprised by this allegation. 'Murdered the owner?'

'Yes, ma'am, so would you please open the boot of the car?' he asked.

The elderly woman walked to the rear of the car and opened the boot, showing it to be empty.

The senior police officer was stunned.

'Is this your car, ma'am?'

'Of course it's my car. Whose do you think it is? Do you want to see my registration documents for it?' she answered.

The officer was confused by this reply.

'One of my officers claims you do not have a driving licence.'

The woman delved into the bottom of her handbag and pulled out her driver's licence and handed it over to him to examine, after which he appeared quite puzzled and unsure about all that had taken place.

As he handed her back the licence, he said, 'Thank you, ma'am. But I was led to believe by one of my officers that you did not have a driver's licence, that you stole this car, that you murdered the owner and that you chopped up his body and stuffed it into plastic bags within the boot.'

The elderly woman gave him a look of pure innocence and, shaking her head, said, 'I bet the bloody big liar told you I was speeding too?'

Honey Come Back!

• • •

When my former colleague Tom Kelly's young daughter Nicola was five years old, she had a hamster called Honey.

Unfortunately, Honey developed a tumour, which was clearly visible on her side, due to the large swelling.

After a family meeting, Nicola and Tom agreed that Honey had to be seen to by the vet.

The following Monday morning, Tom was walking Nicola along the footpath to her school. She was upset and crying, knowing that today was the day that Honey would be taken to the vet, once Tom had left her at the school.

'Daddy, will you promise me you'll take Honey to the doctor's and make sure that she gets medicine to make her well again?' she asked.

Tom immediately responded that he would.

They both stood there for several minutes, Nicola crying and Tom trying to stop his eyes from filling up with tears watching her.

After he left her, Tom collected Honey and took her to the vet.

He confirmed it was a tumour and said it would be kinder for Honey to put her to sleep there and then.

Tom explained his fear of meeting Nicola after school and telling her the news, but reluctantly he had to agree with the vet's professional advice.

Once the deed was done, Tom asked the vet what he owed him for his services.

'Just give me a fiver,' the vet said.

Tom paid him the money and slowly walked out of the surgery, upset, but more importantly, worried about how Nicola would react to the news.

He arrived outside the school gates early and waited nervously for her to come out.

Suddenly, he was alerted by the school bell ringing and looked up to see Nicola running across the school playground towards the gates.

She was wearing a big smile on her face and shouting, 'Daddy, did you get Honey to the doctor? Is she all better now?'

Tom looked down at her innocent little face and said, 'Nicola, Daddy has some bad news for you.'

'Oh, nooooooo, Daddy! What is it?' she screamed, her eyes filling up with tears and the look of sadness written all over her wee face.

There was no easy way to do it; Tom had to tell her straight.

'Nicola, you owe Daddy a fiver!'

The Blackhills of Glesca!

...

Two cops were walking the beat in Blackhill, when they were instructed to attend a complaint regarding a noisy neighbour.

On arrival at the tenement close, they were met with the reporter, who described the noise in her best Glaswegian patter.

'It sounds like he's got a fucking army up there, by the way!'

The cops went to the neighbour's door and were invited inside, where they then related the complaint about the noise to the householder.

'Ah know exactly whit it is,' he said, whereupon he led them to the bathroom, where they discovered he was keeping a horse, with the bath filled with straw and horse manure all over the floor.

The cops were curious to know why he was keeping a horse in the bathroom of his house, to which he replied, 'Ah've got tae keep it in there in case some bastard steals it! Ye cannae leave fuck all outside here.'

'Horse thieves in the Blackhill? Surely not!'

The Best Man

• • •

It just so happened that during the beginning of the Serious Crime Squad, a vacancy arose for a Detective Inspector.

The names of officers applying for the role were whittled down until there were only three candidates left.

A Detective Sergeant from the Metropolitan, a Detective Sergeant from Edinburgh City and a Detective Sergeant David Trimmer from Glasgow.

The promotion panel decided to set them a task, where they would release a brown rabbit into the Pollok Estate Park, and each candidate in turn had to use his persuasive skills and detection ability to track it down, catch it and present it before the panel.

First to go was the DS from the Met. He immediately sought the advice of his former colleagues in New Scotland Yard, whom he had worked with on covert anti-terrorist operations.

After three days in the park, he returned to the promotion panel tired, dejected and empty handed.

Next to go was the DS from Edinburgh. He sought the help and advice of his former colleagues in the Special Branch as to how to go about the task set before him. All of his expert experience gained in covert operations was put into practice, but just like the candidate before him, after three days, he returned to the panel empty handed and admitted defeat.

Last to go was David Trimmer from Glasgow, who contacted two of his old plain-clothes buddies from his shift in the Gorbals for some last-minute advice before he entered the park.

Within twenty minutes of him entering, screams of pain could be heard as David returned to the edge of the park, dragging towards the panel a large brown bear wearing police handcuffs, with the bear yelling, 'OKAY! OKAY! I'M A FUCKING RABBIT!'

Who?

...

A client calls up a lawyer's office and the phone is answered, 'Jakobsen, Jakobsen, Jakobsen and Jakobsen Solicitors, can I help you?'

'Can I speak with Mr Jakobsen please?' the client asks.

'I'm sorry but he's on holiday.'

'Well, let me talk with Mr Jakobsen,' he says.

'He's out of the office and won't be back in until Monday.'

'Then put me through to Mr Jakobsen,' he responded.

'He's at court defending a client.'

'Okay then, can I talk to Mr Jakobsen?'

To which the person answering the phone replied, 'Speaking!'

What's Up Doc?

· · ·

This is one of those stories you hear, and think must be a joke, but it isn't: this actually happened and was in the news.

Apparently a driving instructor, trying to boost his macho appearance, stuck a large carrot down the front of his trousers and pretended it was his erect penis.

Whilst behaving like this, he groped three female learner drivers in a series of indecent attacks.

Having received several complaints, he was arrested and appeared in court where he was found guilty of two indecent assaults and two sexual assaults.

On one occasion, having placed a ten-inch carrot down the front of his trousers, he told one of his driving school pupils that she had executed a manoeuvre so good, it had given him an erection.

He then took her hand and made her touch the vegetable, before revealing later, during her lesson, that it was just a carrot.

He admitted to a jury that it was totally unprofessional, stupid and he now regretted doing it.

The court also heard that he had offered to waive the driving fees of a pupil who had failed her test, if she would pull over into a lay-by and perform oral sex on him. She refused.

'Oral sex with a carrot? NO THANKS, JASPER!'

No doubt he tried to convince her of the old wives' tale about carrots being good for your eyesight and helping you to see better in the dark. But so do Specsavers, and they're doing a better deal: 'Buy one pair, get another pair free!'

Anyway, it does conjure up a whole new meaning to your Sunday lunch of 'MEAT AND TWO VEG' being good for you!

Barking Mad
• • •

I once attended at a house regarding a complaint about dogs continually barking.

On my arrival at the house I was invited in by the owner, amid the noise of several dogs barking.

I informed him why I was there and he explained to me that his dog had recently had pups and within the following week they would all be away to new owners, having been purchased in advance.

He then led me through to a room to view the dogs, who were all hyperactive.

'Get down, Rolex. Ebel, come here! Sit down, Timex. Cartier! Stop chewing that cushion!'

I looked on with interest before asking the inevitable.

'So what kind of dogs are they then?'

To which he looked at me and said, 'I thought that would be obvious to you, Officer! They're watch dogs!'

Spartacus

• • •

I was reading an article in the Police magazine recently, where the infamous scene from the Hollywood epic blockbuster *Spartacus* was recreated. Two detective police officers from the same area, with the same name, were assigned to investigate a burglary case, and it just so happened that when they interviewed the potential suspect involved, by sheer coincidence, he also shared the same name.

Both detective officers were less than keen to claim his identity.

It makes you want to dig deeper to see if the detectives were in fact related to the suspect as well!

Only joking, guys!

That famous scene in the film is where the Romans have captured Spartacus and all his men and make them the offer that if the real Spartacus identified himself, then the rest of his men would be spared a horrible death.

The macho Kirk Douglas (Spartacus) sits with John Ireland and a young Tony Curtis and tells them that the only thing left for him to do is to stand up and admit to his identity, thereby sparing them all from a horrible, drawn-out death.

After several deep-breathing exercises, he gets to his feet and utters the immortal words, 'I'm Spartacus!'

But, to his surprise, and a good bit of scriptwriting, one by one his loyal army of brave men get to their feet and do likewise, each one proudly declaring, 'I'm Spartacus! I'm Spartacus! I'm Spartacus! I'm Spartacus!'

Now, as touching as this scene is, if it was moved to modern-day Glasgow, there would be no chance of that ever happening.

Picture the scene once more. Kirk Douglas gets to his feet, and admits to his identity. 'I'm Spartacus!'

The others in his gang follow his lead and immediately stand up in support of him, and within a few seconds their arses would be making buttons whereby they would instantly point their accusing fingers at him, positively identifying him to the police officers present.

'He's Spartacus!', 'He's Spartacus!', 'That bastard there sir!', 'He made us dae it!', 'Ah didnae mean it!', He's Spartacus and I'm a crown witness!', 'Ah saw him dae whatever you want me tae say he did!'

Fact or Fiction?

• • •

The brief scenario is as follows.

Young Billy has just broken the window of the next-door neighbour's car.

Back in the 1960s, Billy's dad would have dragged him into the house and leathered his arse with a carpet beater, after which he would have reimbursed the neighbour for the cost of his replacement car window.

Billy would be more careful in the future, grow up a normal, respectable boy, study hard at school, go on to college and become a successful businessman.

But present-day Billy would call Childline and report his dad. As a result of his phone call, his dad would be arrested for child abuse.

Billy is subsequently removed from the family home and taken into foster care, where he stays out late at night and joins a gang.

A psychologist visits the family and informs Billy's sister that she remembers also being abused by their dad.

As a result of his report, the dad goes to prison.

Billy's mum finds it difficult living alone, being a single parent, and ends up having an affair with the psychologist.

The psychologist gets a promotion!

Fact or fiction?

Wrong Side of the Bed

· · ·

Mother Superior was on her way to the late-morning prayers, when she passed two novices just leaving early-morning prayers and on their way to classes.

As she passed them, she said, 'Good morning, ladies.'

The novices replied, 'Good morning, Mother Superior. May God be with you.'

After she had passed them, she heard one say, 'I think she got out of the wrong side of the bed this morning!'

This remark startled her, but she chose to ignore it.

Further along the corridor, she passed by two of the Sisters who had been teaching at the convent for several years. She greeted them as normal with the words, 'Good morning, Sister Martha, Sister Jessica, may God flood your minds with wisdom for our students today.'

'Thank you, Mother Superior, and may God be with you.'

Again, after passing, she overheard the words, 'She got out of the wrong side of the bed today.'

Puzzled by this, she started to wonder if she had spoken harshly, or displayed an irritated look on her face. So she vowed to be more pleasant.

Looking further along the corridor, she saw retired Sister Mary approaching, step by step, with her walker. Knowing that she was slightly deaf, Mother Superior had plenty of time to put on a pleasant smile before greeting her.

'Good morning, Sister Mary. I'm so happy to see you up and about. I pray the Lord watches over you and gives you a wonderful day!'

Sister Mary looked at her closely and said, 'Ah, good morning, Mother Superior, and thank you. I see you got out of the wrong side of the bed this morning!'

Mother Superior was totally stunned by this.

'Sister Mary, please tell me. What have I done wrong? I have gone out of my way to be pleasant and greet everyone with a smile, but three times already today people have made the same remark about me.'

Sister Mary stopped with her walker and turned to face her.

'Oh, don't take it personal, Mother Superior. It's just that you're wearing Father Jack's boots!'

Glesca Bomb Alert

...

During the late seventies and early eighties in Glasgow, we were to receive a large number of Bomb Alerts at the police office, with regards to 'bombs' within certain public houses.

Apart from one that I personally attended, which was genuine and did blow up, the rest of them were hoax calls, but we still had to attend and carry out the police procedure methods, as detailed in our instruction manual, of how to approach and deal with such an incident.

However, Glasgow and the people who reside there are not like the inhabitants of any other city – particularly when it comes to asking them to part company with alcohol!

It would be true to say you would have more chance of them parting company with the wife and weans!

One call in particular, on a Friday night, referred to a well-established public house that was so overcrowded, it was bursting at the seams – or, as we say in Glesca, it was heavin'!

Accompanied by my colleagues, I entered the premises and made my way to the bar to seek out the landlord of the establishment, to inform him of the bomb threat call, and the need to evacuate the premises forthwith.

I then proceeded to inform the patrons in the pub of the need for their co-operation with regards to our presence there and to calmly make their way in an orderly fashion outside onto the street while we made a thorough search of the premises.

This request did not go down well with the majority of the patrons, who refused point-blank to leave, citing the following reasons:

'But I've just bought a round up for the table, big man!'

'That pint has just been poured afore you came in and I'm no' leaving it for some other bastert tae swally while I'm hanging about outside!'

'Can ah get a quick whisky, Officer? I've got tae go up the road, my tea will be on the table!'

They just would not accept the fact that someone would try to bomb their pub!

So much so that even the pub landlord refused to leave.

Not to be compared with the Captain of a sinking ship.

Not at all.

And it was certainly nothing to do with bravery in any shape or form by the landlord.

His excuse for not leaving his premises was the fact that every bugger who went outside the pub during the evacuation would return and immediately complain about how their round of drinks, bought just prior to being asked to leave the premises, had mysteriously disappeared, or been drunk by someone else, or spilled during their absence.

Therefore he remained to guard all the drinks in the place!

In some premises, a bomb hoax call was becoming a regular occurrence for the patrons and an expensive round of drinks, in the aftermath, for the pub landlords!

It was also discovered to be part of a ploy by some pub patrons, after they had witnessed the police procedure on their arrival at such an incident.

However, it was after a police controller received three bomb alert calls on the one night to a certain pub in the east end of Glasgow that a trace was done on where the hoax calls had been made from and it was confirmed.

They had all been made from the public telephone inside the pub.

Some people will go to any length to scam a free drink!

Airport Alert

· · ·

Airport baggage handler/terrorist attack hero/local celebrity John Smeaton and one of his baggage handler colleagues, Fred, are celebrating at a party for John's new-found fame as the hero of the Glasgow airport terrorist attacks.

After a few beers and one or two whiskies, they hear one of their colleagues mention that aircraft fuel gives cocktails an extra kick.

Just what is needed to keep the party swinging along nicely!

So they help themselves to some of this fuel to liven up the party.

Sure enough, the cocktails with the added kick of aircraft fuel taste great, and everybody at the party is swallowing it down, faster than a speeding Jeep through the doors of the airport.

As a result, they all get totally rat arsed!

The following day, John is awakened by the phone ringing.

When John answers the phone his mate Fred calls out, 'John! John!'

'What is it, Fred?'

'How are you feeling after your fuel cocktail?' Fred asks.

'Not bad at all,' John replies.

'Well tell me this then. Have you farted at all this morning?' Fred asks.

'Not yet!' John replies. 'Why do you ask?'

'Because for fuxsakes, don't,' Fred shouts. 'Cause I just did, and I've ended up in Palma Mallorca!'

The Final Orgasm!

...

An elderly lady in Edinburgh contacted the police control room in Glasgow, stating that she had spent the previous night and most of the morning trying to contact her daughter who resided in the Partick area, without any success, and as a result of this she was becoming anxious with regards to her health.

The history was that the daughter, a mature student who lived alone and studied at the University of Glasgow, suffered from an ongoing heart complaint.

As a result, during my police patrol, I was instructed to attend the home address and check it out.

On arrival at the house, I could see that the living-room curtains were closed.

I knocked on the door several times, but got no answer. Whilst I was doing this, my colleague Dick Waddell had gone to the rear of the house and looked in the window.

Moments later he returned and said, 'I think we have a sudden death here!'

At that, we forced the door and entered the house, and as we went into the living room we discovered the daughter, lying naked, face down over a foot stool, with the TV still on.

We could also hear a distinct buzzing sound.

Dick went around the room, switching off the television, the lamp, the fire, but still there was a buzzing noise. Then suddenly we realised it was coming from the deceased female.

On closer inspection, we discovered she had a vibrator

sticking out of her private parts, and it was still going strong.

Duracell batteries, no doubt!

This prompted Dick to switch the TV back on immediately and play the video recorder, and we then discovered she had been watching a blue movie prior to her death.

It appears, according to the police casualty surgeon that she had become so excited while watching the movie that she had unfortunately suffered a massive heart attack, which was to prove fatal.

After making the necessary arrangements and obtaining enough information for a report, Dick instructed the police in Edinburgh to call at her elderly mother's home and deliver the death message, although we made no mention of how she was found, in order to spare her embarrassment.

So a word of warning to all you ladies out there: if you ever decide to behave in this way, just make sure your heart is in good condition – and remember, that banging at the door just might be a police officer, sent by your mother to check you're alright!

Drink!
. . .
One Tequila, two tequila, three tequila, FLOOR!

Devine Intervention
· · ·

It's amazing, but nobody ever makes a complaint about a man of the cloth.

For example, having received a call from the local priest, regarding him retaining a youth whom he had just caught spray-painting graffiti on the chapel wall, a panda car was despatched to attend.

On their arrival at the manse, the officers were invited in by the housekeeper, and offered some tea or coffee.

The officers explained their reason for attending and the housekeeper said, 'I'm making it for Father Devine, so you might as well join him, he'll be back in a minute!'

Father Devine appeared and sat down with the officers to enjoy his tea, during which he told the officers about what had occurred. He added that they were not to rush their tea; he wasn't going anywhere.

'So where is he now?' one of the officers asked, intrigued by the priest's casual attitude.

'He's just outside in the garage waiting for you!' Father Devine said.

The priest then led them into the garage, where they found the ned with his hands tied behind his back with cord, and a rather colourful tie round his neck, placed there by the priest, and trapped in the passenger-door window of his car to prevent him from escaping.

Knife, Fork And Yuck!

. . .

This is a story with a timeless lesson on how consultants can make a difference to an organisation and it's aimed at all of you diners out there who frequent restaurants and understand the need for the service to be faster and more efficient.

Last week several police officers on a shift night out booked a table at a new restaurant.

Whilst perusing the menu, it was obvious that the waiter noting down the meal order was carrying a spoon in his breast shirt pocket.

It appeared a little strange.

However, when another waiter approached the table with a jug of water and some utensils, he too had a spoon in his shirt pocket.

As they looked around the restaurant, they saw that all the waiting staff had spoons in their breast shirt pockets.

When the waiter returned to serve the first course of soup, one of the cops asked, 'Why the spoon in your pocket?'

'Well!' the waiter replied. 'The restaurant owner hired a consulting agency to revamp all our processes with regards to time and motion, and after several months of analysis, they concluded that the spoon was the most frequently dropped utensil and it represents a dropped frequency of approximately three spoons per table, per hour.

Therefore, if the restaurant personnel are better prepared, we can reduce the number of trips back to the kitchen and save at least twelve man hours per shift!'

As luck would have it, one of the cops dropped his spoon and the waiter was able to replace it immediately with his spare one.

'I'll get another spoon the next time I go to the kitchen, instead of making an extra trip to get one right now.'

The cop was impressed, but also noticed that there was a string hanging out of the waiter's trouser fly.

Then, looking around the room, he noticed that all of the waiters had a string hanging from their trouser fly. So, before he walked off, the cop asked him, 'Excuse me, but can you tell me why you all have that string dangling from your trouser fly?'

'Certainly, sir!' Then he lowered his voice. 'Not everyone is as observant as you, but the same consulting agency I mentioned to you earlier also discovered that we can save time in the restroom by tying this piece of string on to the tip of your penis, and you use the string to pull it out from your trousers without having to touch it, thereby eliminating the time needed to wash your hands and, as a result, shortening the time spent in the restroom by almost eighty per cent.'

The cop thought about what he had been told and then asked, 'So after you have taken your penis out, how do you put it back inside your trousers?'

'Well!' the waiter whispered. 'I can't speak for the others, but I personally use the spoon!'

Jackie Wilson Said

• • •

Two old guys were reminiscing with some of the younger guys in the pub, telling stories from their past, about the time when they were at the height of their career as a couple of thieves, but more commonly referred to as 'housebreakers'.

No one's premises were safe with these two old codgers residing in the area nearby, and double glazing, alarms and the odd watch dog were not a guaranteed deterrent for them either.

However, the men were relating a story about where it had gone wrong, for a change!

Apparently they had set a plan to break into a newsagents' shop and steal a large haul of cigarettes, tobacco and the contents of the small money safe at the rear of the shop.

Everything went like clockwork, as they silenced the alarm system with foam prior to entering the shop, then once inside they filled their bags with the goodies they came for, along with the proceeds from the safe.

Leaving the premises by the same route, they were about to walk back out onto the street and disappear, when Jackie stopped George in his tracks and said, 'Get back, George!'

George immediately reacted to Jackie's warning.

'What is it, Jackie?' he asked.

'There's a couple of plainclothes coppers sitting in a motor outside. They must have got a tip off and are sitting watching the place!' Jackie replied.

'What will we do?' George asked.

Jackie thought for a moment, trying to think of an answer.

'There's nothing else for it. We'll just have to wait them out and hope that they get fed up sitting about and leave.'

Both men concealed themselves behind some boarding as they played the waiting game with the police officers in the car outside.

Almost an hour later, and beginning to suffer from the early cold morning, Jackie decided to pop his head out and take a look to see what was happening, but the disappointment was etched across his face as he turned to George.

'The bastards are still there, sitting in their fancy motor. Probably got the heating up full as well, while we're out here freezing our balls off!'

'Maybe they're sleeping, Jackie?' George said.

'Nae chance! I can see the back of their heids; they're both sitting upright!'

Nearly three hours later, it was starting to get light, but they were still hiding behind the boarding with their haul, freezing with the cold, with Jackie periodically checking to see if the police were still staking out the shop.

'Ah cannae believe I'm sitting here freezing my arse off, with a bag full of fags and tobacco and I cannae even have a smoke!' George said, unable to light up in case the cops saw the smoke.

'What time is it now?' Jackie asked.

George checked his watch.

'Twenty past five! How, have you got work tae go tae?' he replied jokingly.

'Naw! But the paper man has and he'll be arriving soon tae open his shop, totally unaware that we've already opened it up for him and helped ourselves tae all of his snout!'

'Shit! So he will. We better GTF afore he arrives,' George said. 'Take another look out and see what they're doing!'

Jackie checked out front, before announcing the bad news.

'Still there! Ye'd think they would give up!' he said. Then he added, 'There's only one thing for it. We dump the fags and walk out like nothing's happened.'

'What! A' the fags?' George replied.

'Aye, a' the fags. Then, if they stop us, we've got nothing on us,' said Jackie.

Reluctantly, they left their haul of fags and tobacco and casually walked out, past the police car, where Jackie gave a fleeting glance to the side before exclaiming, 'Bastard!'

What he'd thought was a police car with two plain-clothed police officers inside turned out to be an ordinary family car with two upright headrests in the front seats.

Jackie looked round at a bewildered George and stated apologetically, 'Honest tae fuck, George. I thought they were coppers from the back!'

Their immediate thought was to return to the rear of the shop and regain their discarded stash.

Unfortunately for them, timing is everything, and as they were about to do so, the newsagent drove up and stopped outside his shop just in the nick of time, before they could act.

And it was now time for our two tired, freezing, bungling housebreakers to head off, before the shopkeeper discovered the break-in and raised the alarm, whereby real cops would attend.

I believe they have a good laugh about it now, but I bet it wasn't funny at the time!

Freezing cold, tired and empty handed, but worst of all, foiled by two car headrests. That was a first!

Do Your Best
· · ·

An elderly man appeared in court as the accused and was subsequently found 'Guilty' of his crime.

After learning of his criminal record as a habitual offender, the Sheriff gave him a stiff sentence.

'I'll never live long enough to do that!' said the elderly man.

To which the Sheriff replied in a sympathetic voice, 'Well, just do what you can!'

Ze Wrong Answer!

• • •

Robertson was a Stipendiary Magistrate who held this position at the Partick Marine District Court in the early seventies.

He was a man with a reputation for being very fair, but also firm.

One particular day, a proud war veteran and former tank commander in the armoured corps appeared before him.

His name was Stanislaw, a Polish migrant charged with offences relating to breach of the peace and assaulting his wife.

As things stood, it was not looking good for Mr Stanislaw, for he had a record of previous offences for similar acts, and his solicitor was of the opinion that he was looking at a custodial sentence.

The solicitor defending him obtained a background report and ascertained that Stanislaw had settled in Scotland at the end of World War Two, and knowing that the magistrate, Mr Robertson, had a proud war record himself, he asked his client in which section of the military he had served during the war.

'I was in ze tanks division,' Stanislaw proudly announced.

'That's absolutely brilliant!' his solicitor replied. 'For a minute there, I thought you were looking at the jail. Leave this to me; you will walk out of here with probation. No problem!'

The solicitor confidently submitted his plea of 'Guilty',

and then went on to describe his plea of mitigation, summarising his client's antecedents, and promising the court that Mr Stanislaw intended to seek counselling for his drink problem and so on, then he threw in the trump card by referring to his client's military service in the armoured corps during the war.

At this, the magistrate's ears pricked up and he enquired, 'The armoured corps, did you say?'

He then indicated for the accused to stand up, which he did immediately.

'Which branch of the armoured corps were you in?' he asked the accused.

Stanislaw immediately came to attention, clicking his heels together and blurted out, loud and clear, 'Ze Panzer Division!'

It appears he had been captured by the Germans at the beginning of the war and, as a result, was forced to serve in the infamous German tank regiment.

Unfortunately, this answer did not go down well with the magistrate, who had proudly served his country during the war, and therefore followed up with the words, 'Sixty days! Take him away.'

Family Values

· · ·

My old mate Ian Taylor was working in the Easterhouse area of Glasgow, and one day he called at a house there while in possession of an arrest warrant for a male, believed to be residing at that address.

He knocked on the door and after it was answered by the female householder, he made her aware of the warrant.

The female informed him that the person he was seeking no longer stayed there.

At that, Ian asked if he could check the house for himself.

The female invited him inside and as he entered the hallway he nearly broke his ankle, due to the floorboards having been removed in part of the hallway.

As he entered the living room area, which was very sparsely furnished, he couldn't help but notice a large colour TV situated in a very unusual position in the room, halfway along the back wall.

It was while standing there, looking at the TV, that he could feel eyes on him and casually looked over his shoulder to see a craggy-faced old man staring straight at him through a big hole in the middle of the wall opposite.

Startled by the unexpected appearance of the elderly man, peering at him through the hole, Ian looked at the female for an explanation.

At which point, she threw her arms out to the side and said, 'That's my Da! He's bedridden and his telly broke down yesterday, so we just knocked a hole in the wall wi' a hammer, so that he could watch our TV as well!'

Fore!

· · ·

Four senior police officers were playing their weekly game of golf, and one remarked how nice it would be to wake up on Christmas morning, roll out of bed and, without an argument, go directly to the golf course, meet his buddies and play a round of golf.

His buddies all chimed in.

'Let's do it! We'll make it a priority and figure out a way to meet here, early on Christmas morning.'

Months later, that special morning arrives, and there they all are on the first tee of the golf course.

The first cop says, 'Man, this game cost me a fortune! I had to buy my wife such a huge diamond ring so that she couldn't take her eyes off it.'

The second cop says, 'I spent a packet as well. My wife is at home planning the cruise I promised her. She was up to her eyeballs in brochures when I left.'

The third cop says, 'Well my wife is at home admiring her new convertible sports car and reading the owner's manual.'

They all turn their heads to look at the last cop in the group, who is staring back at them like they have lost their minds.

'I can't believe that you all went to such expense for this game of golf. I just got up this morning, slapped my wife on the arse and said, "Well, darling, Merry Christmas! It's a great morning and I'm right in the mood for some hot sex or a game of golf."'

'So what happened?' his colleagues asked.

To which he replied, 'She turned her back on me and said, "Mind and take a sweater with you!"'

Fact or Fiction?

· · ·

Brief scenario: Tommy won't sit still in class and his behaviour is disrupting all the other students.

Back in the 1960s, Tommy would have been sent to the Headmaster's office and given a good tongue lashing accompanied by six of the belt. After which he would be returned to his class, where he would sit still and not disrupt the class again.

Present day, Tommy would be prescribed huge doses of the drug Ritalin, receive numerous sessions of time-consuming counselling, and be tested for Attention Deficit Disorder. The school would receive extra funding due to his disability, after which he would drop out of school and become a zombie, living on state benefits for the rest of his life!

Fact or fiction?

Don't Think So!

...

With the police promotion exams fast approaching, an ambitious young sergeant was making enquiries as to where he could get his hands on a set of past exam CDs to assist him.

With modern technology at hand, he searched on the internet and very soon found the CDs he required.

However, he encountered some problems when it came to ordering them from the seller, who was none too pleased with the buyer's request, following their rather brief conversation regarding the items.

I'm informed the conversation went along these lines:

'Hello there!' the young sergeant said. 'I was just wondering if it would be possible to lay my hands on some copies of the Fraud papers for a reasonable price?'

'What do you mean by copies?' the seller asked.

'Well I already have the 2007 set and really don't want to have to buy them again, but I need to re-sit my Inspector Part 1 again!' he explained.

To which the seller courteously and understandably replied, 'No! Certainly not! That would be a contravention of the Copyright Laws, and bear in mind your current position as a serving police sergeant. All officers of the law, regardless of their rank, must be of good character, with honesty and integrity.

With all due respect to you, Sergeant, you should be thoroughly ashamed of yourself to even consider asking such a thing of me, and you should know better!'

At that, the telephone was promptly put down.

I wonder if this request to have the discs copied was the reason for him having to sit his test again?

Tut! Tut!

Lucky Jim

• • •

A wild party was going on at the Lochinch Police Social Club and, as per usual, it was well attended.

Over at the end of the bar, seated in his usual position, propping up one end of it, was Jimmy McDermott.

Suddenly the bar door swung open and in walked big Maggie Forbes, a larger than life Force Support Officer, who loudly announced, 'If anybody in the bar can guess my weight, they can sleep with me!'

Jimmy afforded her a fleeting glance through the bottom of his beer glass, while emptying the remaining contents down his throat, then blurted out sarcastically, 'You're about 92 stone, ya fat ugly cow!'

Quick as a flash, Maggie grabbed hold of his arm, yanked him off his stool and said, 'That's close enough for me, ya lucky bastard!'

The Robbing Mail

· · ·

There was an 83-year-old widow from Paisley, who lived alone, surviving on her state pension. As it was coming up to Christmas, she decided for a change to invite her two sisters over and make the festive turkey dinner, thereby securing some welcome company. However, on her way to the shops, someone had stolen her purse containing the £50 she had saved to pay for this special occasion.

As a woman of simple faith, she sent off a handwritten letter to God, explaining her predicament and seeking his divine help.

A few days later her letter duly arrived on the desk of the manager for the Royal Mail sorting office, whose main job was to deal with 'undeliverable' mail such as this.

As he read over the elderly widow's letter, he was touched by her tragic story and decided to help her out, along with some of his fellow workers within the sorting office, who had also been moved by her letter. They had a whip round and collected a fair amount of money.

They then placed the proceeds from their collection into an envelope and posted it through her letterbox as a surprise.

Several days after Christmas, the sorting office manager was back at work, sifting through the mail, when he came across another letter addressed to God and recognised the handwriting as that of the elderly widow. He quickly summoned his colleagues to gather round while he read it out.

The letter read as follows:

'Dear God, How can I ever thank you enough for what you did for me? Due to your kind generosity, I was able to put on a wonderful festive dinner for my sisters to enjoy and we had a lovely day together. Kind regards, Daphne Brown.

PS. By the way, God, there was £4 missing from the envelope. I'm pretty sure it was those robbing bastards at the post office!'

You're Booked

• • •

It's hard to believe that pop singer/performer Alvin Stardust wasn't a bigger star, when you learn that his agents were those well-known stars of TV entertainment, Reggie and Ronnie Kray!

Just Like Amy

. . .

A senior cop was out on patrol with a young police probationer the other night and she was chatting about her taste in music.

It turned out her favourite singer just happened to be Amy Winehouse.

The senior cop screwed up his face and told her that while he was over in New York on annual leave that year, he had managed to obtain tickets to go to the David Letterman Show and it just so happened that Amy Winehouse was the guest singer.

The probationer appeared very envious of him, but he told her that he didn't know what the Americans would have thought of her with her 60s beehive hairdo.

He also described how she was wearing a black slimline sleeveless dress which showed off her Popeye the sailor tattoos on her arms to the full.

He then went on to say that he was personally disgusted with her and that he hated tattoos on a woman.

'What makes them do it? Scarring their skin for life and then they end up regretting it when they are older after it has lost its colouration and cannot be removed, unless you have lots of money to pay for expensive, painful laser treatment.'

All the while, the young probationer sat there listening to him ranting, without interrupting him or attempting to argue back.

At the completion of their shift, she was leaning over the rear seat while getting out their equipment and her vest rode up at the back, along with her blouse, revealing a large, colourful, ornate tattoo across her lower back.

Oops!

Pension Day
. . .

A retired cop returned home after having been out to buy a few messages for the house.

'What kept you? You've been away for ages!' said his wife.

'It was that new lassie in the post office; she made me show her the grey hairs on my chest before she would give me my pension!' he replied.

His wife responded by saying, 'You should have showed her your willy, and she might have given you disability benefit at the same time!'

Car Boots

• • •

Walking through a car boot market the other day, I stopped to peruse a stall and the articles on display.

While browsing through some of the junk I came upon an old mobile phone, often referred to as a 'brick' due to its size and old-fashioned shape.

'How much for this?' I asked the elderly stallholder in a foreign-sounding accent, while holding it up.

'It's a mobile phone!' she replied.

I knew that instantly on picking it up, for it was like comparing a new digital radio with an old valve wireless.

'I know it's a mobile phone, I'm asking how much?'

'Eh! Give me a pound,' she said.

'Does it work?'

'Of course it works. It just needs charged.' At that, she handed me a large black plug-in charger, even bigger than the phone.

I fiddled about with the phone, trying to switch it on, but to no avail.

'It's not switching on.'

'Well it was,' she said unconvincingly. 'Here, let me see it.'

She took possession of it and started pressing all the buttons for a few moments, then said, 'It was working a minute ago. It'll just need charged! Take it for fifty pence.'

Now I'm really on the wind up, so I ask her, 'How do you work camera? So I can take pictures and send them home.'

'What camera? It doesn't have a camera,' she replied.

'So how do you take pictures?' I asked her in all seriousness.

'You don't! It's a mobile phone, no' a bloody Polaroid.'

'So you not take pictures with it?' I said in my fake broken English.

'No, you can't take pictures . . . But you can use it to phone a friend to come round and take pictures for you!' she said, winking at the stallholder next to her, bringing some humour into the situation.

'But the phone, it doesn't work,' I said, reminding her.

'Well borrow somebody else's phone to call them while you charge that one up!' Then she turned and mumbled out of the side of her mouth, 'Frigging hell, I think I must attract them.'

So I stood there, turning it backwards and forwards as if I was examining it, but looking confused and I could feel her eyes penetrating me as I did, so I thought I'd lead her on a wee while longer.

'Has it got MP3 player?'

'What in hell's name is an empty three player?' she asked, exasperated by my latest question.

'No! Not empty three player, but MP3 player,' I said. 'Music! I want to hear music!'

'Och, it's a bloody stereo you want, no' a phone!' she replied, before turning to the nearby stallholder and whispering, 'Fucking two minutes in the country and they're already trying to educate us. Next he'll be running my stall and I'll need to pay him just to take my stuff!'

I could hear her talking, so I said to her, 'I might be foreign person, but I not deaf!'

'I never said you were daft, ya bam! I said you no understand the lingo very well, that's all!' she responded, trying to back track, but not very convincingly.

'What is lingo? Does phone have lingo?' I asked.

'Oh definitely, and it's got it in colour as well. None of your black and white shite, but full colour, all for fifty pence cash! No paying it up, either. Cash only!'

'It has TV screen?' I said.

'TV and the full Sky package with all the premier films and all for fifty pence!' she replied sarcastically.

'How many channels?' I asked.

'Full package, I told you! Are you no' listening, or are your ears painted on?'

I paused for a moment, screwing up my face as if trying to understand, then I asked her, 'You are giving me fifty pence to take phone?'

She looked at me, then scratched her head and said, 'You know something, son, it would be worth giving you fifty pence just to get rid of you.'

She then started to rummage about in her money bag until she found a fifty-pence piece and, handing it over to me, she said, 'Here, son, take that and piss off and annoy somebody else!'

I looked at her, puzzled, and said, 'How much are ye wanting for yer phone hen, afore a piss aff?'

She stared at me, unsure for a moment, then said, 'Ya big bastard! You've been winding me up and I believed you were a refugee. Ya bastard!'

I started to laugh and was soon joined by the female in the next stall, and as I looked back at the stallholder, she said with a straight face, 'If you want the phone, it's back up to a pound, Mr smart arse!'

Home Made Soup

...

An old man contacted the police after returning home to discover his house had been broken into.

The police attended at his house and obtained the necessary details for their report.

As it was, nothing had been stolen, but the suspects had vandalised several items within the house.

'So, you're definitely sure there is nothing missing from the house?' the cop asked.

'Nothing! Not a thing. Just some damage,' replied the old man, before adding, 'Although some dirty bastard did a big toley in a pot of soup I'd just made . . .'

Then he paused for a moment before adding, 'I've had to throw half of it out!'

Renovation Time

· · ·

I've just bought a new house and I've been renovating it along with my brother Hughie.

The other day, along with Hughie, I had to attend at a female friend's house who was advising me on my finances.

'Have you a lot of work to do to it?' she asked Hughie.

Hughie replied that he was having to strip the wallpaper off all the walls in the house.

There was a pause for a few moments before she asked Hughie, 'Do you have a steamer?'

To which Hughie responded by saying, 'I do! But I didn't think you'd notice it under these overalls!'

True Fact!

· · ·

Dr Harvey Kellogg intended his first breakfast cereal product to be an antidote for masturbation. Personally, I prefer porridge!

Moral of the Story

· · ·

Whilst at Tulliallan Police College, one of the instructors asked the class to think of a story that has a moral.

Ricky Gray was the first to go and said, 'Last week when I was driving my mother back from the farmers' market, she was holding onto a basket of eggs, and suddenly I hit a bump in the road causing some of the eggs in her basket to break.

'The moral of my story is: don't put all your eggs in one basket!'

'Very good, Ricky,' the instructor said. 'Okay, who's next?'

Maggie Mulligan stood up and said, 'My granddad kept chickens and put five of their eggs into an incubator, but only three of them hatched out.

'The moral of my story is: never count your chickens until they're hatched!'

'Again, very good,' responded the instructor. 'Next.'

Jimmy Clark got to his feet and said, 'My wife's uncle Bert was in Afghanistan when his helicopter was shot down and crashed behind enemy lines. All he had in his possession was a machine gun, his army knife and a case of Stella Artois beers.

'He quickly drank down all the beers before shooting twenty-four Taliban. Then he ran out of bullets, so he stabbed another fifteen with his knife. Then his knife blade broke, so he strangled another six with his bare hands, before plotting his escape across dangerous terrain to safety!'

There was silence for a few moments, before the instructor asked Jimmy, 'So what is the moral of your story then?'

To which Jimmy replied, 'Simple! The moral of my story is: don't fuck with the wife's Uncle Bert when he's drunk!'

True Fact!

. . .

In Iran in 1994 Mohammad Esmail al-Bahrami, aged 105, filed for divorce from his wife, Fatemeh Razavi, aged 100.

Apparently his mother warned him it would never last!

Wednesday Shopping

· · ·

Wednesday is shopping day. It's the day I take my elderly mother out for her messages to Morrison's superstore, followed by some lunch before I take her back home.

As we were walking round the store, she asked, 'Gonnae go and see if they have my Dutch Crispbake biscuits in this week. They didnae have them last week and I ended up buying they bionic ones, they're bloody disgusting, it's like eating cardboard! I ended up handing them in to Isobel next door. She likes awe that bionic stuff.'

'It's organic, not bionic!' I said, correcting her.

'Och, it's the bloody same thing, you know what I mean!'

Off I went to look for her biscuits, returning a few minutes later with the news that there were none on the shelf.

'Aw that's a bloody disgrace. They're at it in here. I've no' managed to get them for a few weeks now,' she said.

Then she spotted a store supervisor. 'Excuse me, son, but where are your Dutch Crispbake biscuits?' she asked in a soft, plausible old lady's voice. 'Cause I don't see them, son, and you didnae have them in last week either! In fact, I ended up buying those bionic ones, but they're absolutely tasteless.'

'I'm very sorry, dear, but we have none in stock, and there's none at the warehouse either, so it's only the organic ones we have in stock, but we're waiting for an order to come in any day,' he replied apologetically.

'Aw that's good, son, 'cause I miss them. Thanks for

that!' she said with a smile on her face. Then as the supervisor walked off, she turned to me and her expression changed and she said, 'What a bloody liar! A big store like this and they don't have any Dutch biscuits! He's at it! Probably got boxes of them in the back shop, but he's trying to get rid of that bionic crap first!'

I just shook my head at her and said, 'Organic, Mam. Organic!'

All My Life's a Circle

• • •

Two youths were found guilty of drug abuse and, as it was their first offence, the Sheriff decided to be lenient towards them, so he sentenced them both to go out onto the streets and convince other youths about the evils of taking drugs.

Two weeks later, they were back in court to report to the Sheriff as to how they each got on.

The first youth proudly announced that he had persuaded ten youths to give up drugs, by showing them a piece of paper with two circles thereon, a big one and a smaller one.

He explained to them that the big circle represented the size of their brain before drug abuse, and the smaller circle was the size of their brain after drug abuse.

The Sheriff was very impressed. He turned to the second youth and asked, 'And how many young people have you managed to convert?'

The second youth blurted out ecstatically, 'Two hundred and thirty, m'lord, with many more to follow!'

'Holy shit!' responded a surprised Sheriff. 'And just how did you manage to do that, young man?'

The youth replied, 'It was relatively easy m'lord! I just used the same principle of the two circles.'

Then pointing to the smaller one of the two, he said, 'I told them, this is the size of your arsehole before you go into prison!'

Disastarrgghhh!

...

One of the great things I liked about being a police motor-cyclist was the fact that you were allowed to work by your-self, unsupervised.

However, there came the odd occasion where disaster struck, and never more so than the day I had to escort a chapter of the Orange Lodge from Maryhill to Blythswood Square, and congregate with other lodges, to form their annual parade.

Having started them off on their march, after fifteen to twenty minutes I got bored with the slow pace we were marching at, so I decided to slip away and bugger off home for a short break and some much needed bacon and egg.

As it was, I lived in the Clarkston area, on the south side of the city, the complete opposite side of the river from where I was working.

I decided to take the chance that I wouldn't be missed and, about a mile from my home, I stopped off to buy some morning rolls and a newspaper.

On doing so, I parked immediately behind a large delivery van, and as I dismounted my motorcycle, putting it up onto its stand, I extended my flashing blue light in order to warn oncoming traffic that I was parked, stationary.

It was while I was standing within the queue in the newsagents' shop, with my rolls and newspaper in my hand, and looking out of the window, that I saw the driver of the large delivery van return to his vehicle, jump into his cabin, start up his engine, engage gear and promptly reverse backwards over the top of my police motorcycle.

This was one particular incident that took an awful lot of explaining to the Road Patrol Inspector, as to why I just happened to be parked over on the south side of the city when I was meant to be some twelve miles away, on the north side, escorting the Maryhill chapter of the Orange parade, en route to their city-centre rendezvous.

Fortunately, the Road Patrol Inspector who attended the incident had a good sense of humour, and was more relieved that I hadn't decided to change the route of my Orange parade and take them along with me for the ride!

Two Babysitters?

...

Tayside police received an urgent call regarding a violent male causing a serious disturbance in the main street.

Quick as a flash, two keen young officers, who just happened to be in the police station when the call came in, grabbed a set of car keys off the sergeant's desk and ran out the door to the yard.

As they entered the yard full of vehicles, they pressed the remote control and saw a rather flash-looking unmarked car responding to their signal.

Both officers, without the slightest hesitation, jumped into the front of the car and within seconds they were burning rubber as they roared out of the police yard at speed.

All was going well until the previous shift sergeant, about to go off duty, walked out into the yard and discovered his family car had been stolen.

The police controller immediately broadcast a look-out for the sergeant's stolen vehicle.

Within seconds of the broadcast going out, a mobile station responded, and informed the controller of its subsequent recovery.

Apparently the eager young officers attending the disturbance had unknowingly lifted the sergeant's private car keys from his desk, mistaking them for an unmarked police vehicle in the yard.

However, they had a harder job trying to explain to the sergeant just how they had managed to miss the obvious clues available to them – such as the pink furry dice, a baby seat in the rear and a large 'baby on board' sign in the back window!

'Who drives in a car like this?' Over to you, detective!

Eye Got Set Up!

• • •

When John Smith was a young probationary constable, he was performing office duties and was instructed by the Desk Sergeant to go into the police cells in order to clean up a drunken male prisoner who had sustained a head injury and whose face was covered in blood.

The unsuspecting John entered the cell to clean up the drunken male's face, after which he was about to leave the cell when the drunken male shouted out to him, 'Here, Officer! Can you clean this one as well?'

John turned around to see the drunken male standing there with a huge grin on his face, holding his glass eye in his hand, which was dripping with blood.

The prisoner's action was greeted with howls of laughter from the cell passage outside, as the Desk Sergeant and the prisoner turnkey, who were hiding in the cell passage, watching the entire episode, doubled up with hysterical laughter at the surprised expression on young John's face.

I suppose, in all fairness, they were only keeping an eye out for him!

Know You Well

...

On a recent trip to Santa Ponsa in Majorca, Spain, I was reminded of an incident I was involved in on my very first visit.

It was shortly after I had undergone a vasectomy operation that we decided to go there on a family holiday. We were staying at a complex called Madrugada and it had a friendly, compact little bar underneath the apartments.

This particular night, prior to going upstairs to my apartment, I stopped off, dressed in my casual shirt and shorts, for a glass of beer.

It was whilst sitting outside at one of the tables, sipping away on my beer, that I saw this couple coming towards me and I instantly thought I recognised and knew the female.

'Hello there! I know you, don't I?'

At that, the male shook his head, gave a laugh, like it was a regular occurrence being recognised, and walked into the bar to order his drink, while the female stopped to talk to me.

'Do you come from the Govan area of Glasgow?' I asked her.

'No!' she said. 'But I do work in Govan!'

I then thought for a moment: was she a police woman?

'No, I'm not in the police. I'm a nurse, and I work in the Southern General Hospital.'

At that point the penny dropped and I immediately knew who she was. She was one of the nurses whom I recognised from my vasectomy operation.

'You were present at my vasectomy operation! Do you remember me now?' I asked her, in front of several other holiday makers who were sitting at tables and taking an interest in our conversation.

Slightly embarrassed, she remarked, 'Sorry, but I don't think I recognise your face.'

Quick as a flash, I replied, 'I'm not surprised, hen!'

Then, without the slightest hesitation, I jumped up from my chair and dropped my shorts to my ankles.

'Do you recognise me now?' I asked her as howls of laughter rang out from the people sitting nearby.

However, for the sake of my dear wee mammy, I must point out . . .

Mammy, I was wearing pants underneath!

F.orgot, B.ut I.nvestigating

· · ·

Recently I was out for a meal with American friends Dan and Teri, and Teri was relating an incident to me, involving her neighbour Don and his wife Mary.

Whilst in conversation one day, Teri had informed Don of a new restaurant in the area that they had recently dined in, and recommended it to them for the quality of food and the competitive prices.

Don and his wife Mary decided to accept their recommendation and visit the restaurant for themselves.

When Don and Mary entered the restaurant, there was no maitre d' to greet them and direct them to a table. So, after a few moments, Don took it upon himself to find an empty table for two and sat down.

Having perused the menu and decided upon their choice of evening meal, they both sat back and waited for the waitress to come and note their order.

Twenty minutes passed and Don and Mary were still sitting at their table, patiently awaiting the arrival of a member of staff to take their food and drink order from them.

Fed up with having to wait so long and the complete lack of movement being shown by the waiting staff present, Don became very uneasy and slightly agitated.

Several moments later, totally disillusioned by the poor service, Don and Mary left the premises in disgust.

However, what Dan and Teri had neglected to explain to their neighbours was that as part of the cost-cutting exercises introduced by the restaurateur, in order to make it more competitive with other restaurants in the area, they had reduced the number of waiting staff by having the diners go up to the bar to order their drinks themselves, and place their food order at the same time.

Now, with such a simple self-service idea being introduced to restaurant diners, it is puzzling that Don didn't figure it out for himself, nor indeed did he seek out and read the self explanatory notice board. But, more distressing than that, was learning that Don was in fact a former high-ranking and recently retired FBI agent!

Blackhill Tales

· · ·

There was a railway line that used to run along behind the tenement houses in the Blackhill area of Glasgow.

As it reached a certain point on the track, there was a slight uphill gradient, where the train obviously slowed down.

As a result of this regular occurrence, the natives of the area, having read about Jesse James and his gang of outlaws, would deliberately hinder the train's progress even further by greasing the railway tracks with chip pan lard, or discarded motor engine oil.

Whilst the train was negotiating the added obstacles, causing it to slow down considerably, the more sprightly youths in the gang would run alongside the train, before boarding it, sliding open a cargo door and relieving it of several of the big cardboard cartons it was loaded with, throwing them out to the rest of the gang to retrieve at the bottom of the embankment.

After completing their raid, they would jump off the train before it sped up again and rush over to open the stolen cartons to check out their haul.

You can imagine the expressions on their faces when they discovered they had only gone and knocked off packets of sanitary towels, en route for Timothy Whites the chemist!

However, not everybody was disappointed, as later that day the younger kids of the area played Cowboys and Indians. These particular Indians were Apaches. Guess what the weans were wearing around their heads? Exactly! The sanitary towels.

Blackhill: full of black spots with brighter periods everywhere!

The Right of Reply!

· · ·

The following correspondence actually took place between a resident of the Larden area and Lester and Bingley police.

Dear sir/madam/automated answering service,

Having spent the past twenty minutes waiting for someone at Larden police station to pick up a telephone, I have decided to abandon the idea and try emailing you instead. Perhaps you would be so kind as to pass this message on to your colleagues in Larden by means of smoke signals, carrier pigeon or Ouija board.

As I'm writing this email there are eleven failed medical experiments – I think you would refer to them as youths – in West Cornwall Street, which is just off Commercial Street in Larden.

Six of them seem happy enough to play a game which involves kicking a football against an iron gate with the force of a meteorite.

This in turn causes an earth-shattering CLANG, which in turn rings throughout the entire building.

This game is now in its third week and as I am unsure how the scoring system works, I have no idea if it will end any time soon.

The remaining five failed abortions are happily rummaging through several bags of rubbish and items of furniture that someone has so thoughtfully dumped beside the wheelie bins.

One of them has found a saw and is setting about a discarded chair like a demented beaver on speed.

I fear that it's only a matter of time before they turn their limited attention to the canister of Calor gas that is lying on its side between the two bins.

If they could be relied upon to only blow their own arms and legs off, I would happily leave them to it. I would even go so far as to lend them the matches.

Unfortunately, they are far more likely to blow up half the street, and I've just finished decorating the kitchen.

What I would humbly suggest is this:

After replying to this email with worthless assurances that the matter is being looked into and will be dealt with, why not leave it until the one night of the year, probably bath night, when there are no mutants around, then drive up the street in a police panda car before doing a three-point turn and disappearing again.

This will of course serve no other purpose than to remind us what policemen actually look like in their cars!

I trust that when I take my claw hammer to the skull of one of these throwbacks you'll afford me the same courtesy of giving me a four-month head start before coming to arrest me.

I remain sir, your obedient servant,

Tommy Tellthetruth.

The reply:

Dear Mister Tellthetruth,

I have read over your email and understand your obvious frustration at the problem being caused by youths playing in the area and the personal problems you appear to have encountered while trying to contact the police.

As the Community Police Officer for your street, I would like to extend an offer of discussing the matter fully with you.

Should you wish to discuss the matter further, please provide contact details (address / telephone number) and when it would be suitable to call.

Regards,
PC Runaffmyfeet
Community Beat Officer.

The conclusion:

Dear PC Runaffmyfeet,

First of all, I would like to thank you for your speedy response to my original email. It has only taken you 16 hours and 38 minutes. This must be a personal record for the Larden Police Station and rest assured that I will make a point of forwarding these details on to Norris McWhirter for inclusion in his next *Guinness Book of Records*.

Secondly, I was delighted to hear that our street has its very own community beat officer. May I be the first to congratulate you on your covert skills?

In the last five or so years that I have lived in West Cornwall Street, I have never actually seen you.

Do you hide up a tree, or have you gone deep undercover and infiltrated the street gang itself?

Are you the one with the acne and the moustache on

his forehead or the one with a chin like a wash-hand basin?

It's surely only a matter of time before you are head-hunted by MI5.

Whilst I realise that there may be far more serious crimes taking place in Larden, such as smoking in a public place, or being a Muslim without due care and attention, is it too much to ask for a policeman to explain, using words of no more than two syllables at a time, to these little twats that they might want to play their strange football game elsewhere?

For example, the football pitch behind the citadel, or the one at DJs, are both within spitting distance, and might I also be so bold as to suggest that so is the bottom of the Albert Dock.

Should you wish to discuss these matters further you should feel free to contact me on 010 1010. If after 25 minutes I have still failed to answer, I'll buy you a large one in the Dewdrop Inn.

Regards,

Tommy Tellthetruth.

PS, If you think that this is sarcasm, think yourself lucky that you don't work for the cleaning department!

Stop!

• • •

I was out patrolling on my motorcycle one day, when I saw a driver failing to comply with a 'Stop' sign on the road. He drove straight through the junction, narrowly avoiding collision with other traffic.

I immediately gave chase and stopped the vehicle.

On speaking with the driver I said, 'You failed to comply with the "Stop" sign at the junction.'

'Oh, come on,' the driver said. 'Give me a break, I slowed down, didn't I, is that not enough for you?'

I pointed out to the driver that you're not meant to slow down, you're actually meant to stop. That's why it is called a 'Stop' sign.

The driver looked at me with a smug expression on his face and began to remonstrate with me.

'Slow down! Stop! Slow down! Stop! What's the bloody difference, you idiot? They're both the same thing!'

I then ordered him to step out of his car and said I would attempt, in my own way, to explain to him the difference.

The driver shook his head in disgust as he stepped from his car and stood in front of me, waiting for me to give him my explanation.

At which point I drew my police baton and started giving him a 'Rodney King', walloping him repeatedly across the head and body with it.

As a result of my drastic action, he started screaming in agony at being struck, whereupon I said to him, 'Right, now! Do you want me to slow down? Or stop? Slow down? Or stop? It's your choice!'

I think you can guess what his answer was. But you can be sure he learned from that lesson that there was a considerable difference!

Dating Agencies

• • •

A young cop contacted a dating agency with the request to find him the perfect companion to spend the rest of his life with.

'She must be small and neat, with a cute face,' he said. 'And she must love water sports and group activities!'

The agency loaded his request for the perfect mate into their computer.

Several moments later, the computer printed out:

'Marry a penguin!'

Three Amigos

· · ·

During the start of my service, Jimmy Clark and I were joined regularly by David Ball, another young cop who was on our course and we soon became like the 'Three Amigos'.

Being three keen footballers, we socialised quite often and enjoyed each other's company – and that of Whyte & Mackay!

However, David was an awful guy for meeting up with a female and if he dated her more than once, and she smiled at him at least twice in that time, he wanted to marry her.

As it turned out, it suited Clarky and me, 'cause we were always the first names on his guest list at the engagement party, and Clarky always said, 'Keep the receipt for the present, so you can return it and get your money back!' But the best way was to just tie an elastic band to the present and it was back in your possession when you left the party.

I say that because David's engagements never lasted very long, in fact sometimes they were over before the party ended!

As his best friend and confidante, Jimmy Clark would usually talk him out of it and afterwards he'd wink at me and say, 'That's another party guaranteed in a few months' time!'

This would be long enough for David to meet another potential fiancée, and for us to suggest the venue of the party.

After about his third engagement party and his latest wife-to-be had her dreams of marital bliss ruined by his amigos, who had enlightened her with a few porky pies about his sexual preferences, David actually confided in us a few months later about his latest visually impaired blind date!

This was the one, and of that there was no doubt in his mind.

He had met Callie for the first time at his local Kwik Save superstore, where she was employed as a cashier assistant, and, in David's words, 'It was love at first sight for both of us!'

This was serious stuff, made more obvious by his absenteeism at our regular 'Amigo' meetings in the pub.

Jimmy was worried.

It wasn't so much losing a loyal drinking buddy, who hosted good engagement parties, as gaining a potential wife for David that we hadn't chosen, and who would definitely put an end to our weekly drinking sessions and our quarterly social nights, hosted and financed by the latest fiancée's parents!

The date was set for the latest engagement party and no amount of talking by Jimmy could persuade David to do the honourable thing and chuck her!

As it was, we arrived and took our places at the party, next to the bar, or as near as we could get to it, and sat on the floor.

Through all of his engagement parties, I'd never seen David look so happy and content as he was this time. It was sickening and was going to take an awful lot of

Jimmy's velvet-tongued persuasive powers to talk him out of it.

After about a bottle and a half of whisky were consumed by us, Jimmy called out, 'Eureka! I've got it! I know exactly what to say to him.'

'You've came up with a good reason why he should call it off?' I said.

'Well, not really, Harry,' he blurted out in a drunken slur. 'But fuck it, this could ruin us as the Three Amigos! I'm going to have to tell him straight!'

A short time later, David sat down beside us and consumed several large whiskies to catch up, in order to try and comprehend the utter tosh we were spouting from our mouths.

Moments later, the timing was right for Jimmy to give it to him with both barrels blazing.

He wasn't going to spare his feelings, there was too much at stake for us, his best pals, and drinking buddies.

As Jimmy prepared to begin his speech, with both of them sitting on the floor with their backs to the door, I saw Callie approaching.

'Maybe this isn't a good time to talk about it!' I blurted out.

'Don't be daft. There's no time like the present,' Jimmy said.

'Hear! Hear!' echoed David, appearing pished already.

I suppose I could have said something like, 'Hi, Callie,' and raised their awareness to her presence, but . . . Hey, it was a party and I didn't want to spoil the fun and be a party-pooper!

At that, Jimmy began spouting out his fatherly advice to David, unaware that Callie was standing directly behind them, listening to their every word.

'David! You know that we are your best mates? In fact, we're your only mates, right? But I'm trying to spare your feelings when I say this. So don't take it the wrong way, okay?

'It's Callie. She's not for you! I mean, just her name is a dead giveaway – Callie! I think it was Collie! And they've spelt it wrong. She's an absolute dug! In fact, if they ever film a remake of *Lassie*, she could play the lead!'

'And the collar!' David added, jokingly.

'She must be the ugliest burd you've got engaged to yet! And there has been some humdingers over the past few years!'

The words were barely out of Jimmy's mouth, with David sitting there beside him, nodding his head in agreement, when the entire contents of a can of beer were poured over both their heads by – guess who? Collie!

Sorry, Callie! David's ex-fiancé. With her impromptu action she called off the engagement, there and then!

Suffice to say, that was the last engagement party involving David that we were ever invited to.

Last we heard, he was happily married with five children!

Harry's Police Contacts Page

· · ·

1. Grossly overweight Central Scotland beat man, 42 years old with 23 years' police service and only 3 years away from an ill-health pension, seeks nimble sex-pot, preferably the female variety, for salsa dancing, glasses of tequila, hot chilli nights in with humid screaming passion. Must have own car and willing to travel. Accommodation provided.

Police Box 07/55

2. Very bitter and disillusioned Aberdonian Desk Sergeant, recently dumped by long-term cheating fiancée, seeks a decent, honest, hard-working police-woman, with big tits and long hair, if such a thing still exists in this cruel world of hatchet-faced bitches that look like men, and armed with battery-operated PR24 side-handled batons for company.

Police Box 41/41

3. Artistic Edinburgh woman, 55 years young, ex-Force Support Officer, delightfully plump, anorexic reject, loves eating in/out/here/there and interesting pilau rice dishes and getting caught in the rain, seeks mystic dreamer for romantic nights in and a right good shag . . . pile carpet for my lounge to lie on, in front of a two-bar electric fire with real flame effect while enjoying back rubs. Looks unimportant, visually impaired a bonus. Gagging for it!!!

Police Box 69/69

4. Govan cop, 36 years old, with blue eyes, medium build, brown hair, with a marriage rapidly going down the toilet pan along with my police pension, seeks an alibi for the 26th February, between 6.30–11.45pm.
Police Box 11/45

It's How You Say It!
...

During my induction period within the police, I had to attend Tulliallan Police College for my initial training.

The first morning we had to line up on the parade square, where the fitness and training sergeant performed a roll call of the students present.

This particular Sergeant Jones was Welsh, with a broad, infuriating Welsh accent, which he tended to over-exaggerate.

'TOMP-SON?' . . . 'Here, Sergeant.'

'WIL-SON?' . . . 'Here, Sergeant.'

'MORRI-SON?' . . . 'Here, Sergeant.'

'POY?' . . . 'Here, Sergeant.'

'Is it just POY on its own, or should there be a SON on the end?' he asked, with a smirk on his face.

'No! It's just Poy, Sergeant,' he replied.

'I hope you don't turn out to be a nasty little bugger.'

There was a pause for a moment, before he continued.

'MA-GOORIE?' . . . No reply. 'MA-GOORIE?' . . . No reply. 'I'll come back to you MA-GOORIE!' he said.

'PATER-SON?' . . . 'Here, Sergeant.'

'CLARK-SON?' . . . 'Here, Sergeant.'

'MAL-COL-UM-SON?' . . . 'Here, Sergeant, and it's pronounced Malcolmson.'

At that, he looked up from his parade list, peered over the top of his half glasses, perched on the end of his nose and said, 'That's what I bloody said, MAL-COL-UM-SON, and you answered to it. Now, is that not how you pronounce it, MAL-COL-UM-SON?' he said, with an intimidating stare at Malcolmson.

'Definitely, Sergeant, whatever you say,' Malcolmson replied.

'Don't try and tell me how to pronounce it. It is whatever I say!' he confirmed.

He then paused for a moment to compose himself before continuing.

'MA-GOORIE?' ... Again, no reply. 'If I find out you're here, MA-GOORIE, and not answering to your name, you're in deep shit, irrespective of if you're male or female.'

At that he gave an icy stare to everyone on parade.

'MAC-EE-WAN?' ... Quick as a flash, McEwan replied, 'Here. Sergeant!'

'FEN-WICK?' ... 'Here, Sergeant!'

'BEL- ... BEL-KA ... How the hell do you pronounce your bloody name, BEL-KEE-VITZER?'

'It's Belkevitz! It's Polish, and I'm over here, Sergeant!'

'He looked over at Belkevitz and said, 'Well I knew it wasn't English, so why aren't you over there?'

'My parents emigrated to Scotland, Sergeant!' he responded.

'Well, from now on, I will refer to you as Belky!'

Belkevitz didn't argue with this.

Then, after completing his roll call, he returned to the only name that had not been acknowledged.

'Right, MA-GOORIE! Where are you? I know you're bloody here hiding somewhere, because you ticked your name off on the sheet when you arrived this morning.'

Still there was no reply from the students in the parade.

'Okay then, let's try it another way. Who hasn't heard their name being called out this morning?'

At that, a student in the second row put his hand up.

'You! Step forward. And what's your name, son?' he asked.

'MAGUIRE, pronounced MAG-WIRE, Sergeant!'

'Is that right, Mister MAG-WIRE? Well from now on you will answer to MA-GOORIE, because I think it sounds better, and you look like a MA-GOORIE! Agreed?'

Maguire looked at him for a moment before agreeing to his request, but unfortunately for Maguire, for the rest of his entire police service, he was always referred to as MA-GOORIE!

(Sounds better said with a Welsh accent!)

Motorbiking

• • •

Whilst at Tulliallan Police College I met a colleague from Edinburgh, who told me a story about the time he was asked to perform the duty of a police motorcyclist at the Royal Highland Show.

Although he hadn't attended a motorcycle course, he held a licence to ride one, and as they were very short of motorcyclists for this event, they assigned him for the week.

His duty was to patrol the Newbridge roundabout at the end of the M8 and M9 motorways and monitor the traffic.

In order to perform this duty, he was given a brand new Norton Commando, a wonderful machine that could fairly shift.

After a few hours of patrolling up and down his motorway area, he was instructed to return to the Highland Show for his lunch break, during which, with it being a very hot sunny day, he decided to have a walk round the area.

On returning to his motorcycle, he received a call to assist another officer at a road accident on the roundabout.

With his confidence high, having spent the last three hours riding up and down the motorway on his Norton Commando, he mounted his bike and roared off across the grassy showground with blue lights flashing and siren blaring, as he headed for the exit gate next to the agricultural testing station.

However, as he did so, he was unaware of the metal bar strung across between two poles, placed there to prevent vehicular traffic or the public from entering illegally.

At the last minute, he saw the pole and braked hard, but the bike failed to respond and slid along the grass surface.

Unfortunately for him, he struck the metal pole and was immediately thrown off his bike, but his speeding motorcycle continued on its merry way and collided through the front of a glass greenhouse full of tomato plants and continued to travel along the entire length of it, coming to rest at the opposite end, when it smashed through the glass at the rear.

As a result of the accident, he was conveyed to hospital where it was diagnosed that he had sustained three broken ribs.

However, that was nothing in comparison to the 120 or so trial tomato plants that his runaway bike had destroyed along the way.

He still looks back on this incident and can't fathom why all his applications to join the motorcycle section on a permanent basis were returned to him . . . Application rejected!

The Hypnotist!

. . .

Paul McKenna was booked to appear at the Lochinch Police Club one night to perform his famous hypnotising routine.

He managed to attract several of the audience up onto the stage.

As he whittled them down, he was left with four volunteers, three men and one woman.

One of the men just happened to be my old mate and permanent tormentor, Donnie Henderson.

'Sleep!' said Paul, laying his hand on Donnie's head. 'You're in the desert, it's really hot and you want a drink of water.'

Donnie started licking his lips furiously.

'Now you are at the North Pole,' Paul said. 'And you're freezing your butt off with the cold!'

Donnie started to shiver and rub his arms vigorously.

'Now you're back in Scotland, you have an excellent job in the police, a really nice bungalow in a nice part of Glasgow, a full international Bupa healthcare policy, you drive a top of the range Mercedes, you've recently been promoted to the rank of Detective Superintendent and you're married to an ex-super model!'

At that point, Donnie opened one eye and whispered out of the side of his mouth to Paul, 'If you even attempt to wake me up, I'll fucking jail you!'

Cathy the Cleaner

• • •

One morning, I was over at the Castlemilk Sports Centre with the missus to put in some on the running machine and, when we came out, having carried out a physical work-out that Jane Fonda would have been proud of, we were feeling totally knackered, but dare I say it, completely fit . . . So we went into McDonald's for a Big Mac and chips!

As we sat there loading up with our daily cholesterol intake, my missus was drawn to the cleaner, who appeared to be very thorough in her duties.

It so happened we needed a cleaner to call once, perhaps twice a week, to carry out some general cleaning and dusting in our flat.

This wee woman appeared to tick all the right boxes, according to the missus. Only one more place to check – the toilets!

Having visited the toilets and returned with a glowing report, she told me to call her over and ask her if she was interested in a little extra cash cleaning for us.

After a brief meeting with her, we arranged that she would be picked up by me in the car and driven over to the house, where instead of the £4 per hour she was earning with McDonald's, we would pay her £6 per hour.

By the way, Ronald McDonald wasn't picking her up and dropping her back off afterwards.

As it was, on the Thursday of the same week, I picked her up and brought her to the house.

'Okay, Cathy, I'll leave you to see for yourself what needs

to be done, but it's all the usual things, like mirrors, dusting, emptying the dishwasher, hoovering . . . You'll know what to do, I'm sure!'

As for me, I retired out of the way to my office to do some writing and leave Cathy the cleaner to do the needful.

After about an hour, I went through to see how things were going and, to my surprise, there was Cathy standing outside on the balcony, puffing on a cigarette, and there was the missus hoovering away in the lounge.

I shook my head and returned to my office to carry on with my work, only to return to the kitchen some thirty minutes later to make a coffee, and lo and behold, there was Cathy in the kitchen, sitting at the table, supping away on a cup of tea, and the missus was in the bedroom, polishing the mirrored wardrobes.

I might be slow, but I quickly assessed the situation and came up with the answer: something isn't right here!

I walked from the kitchen with my coffee at the same time as Cathy was going back outside to the balcony for another intake of nicotine.

About an hour later, I again walked through to the kitchen to find Cathy rearranging the glasses in the cabinet, shortest to the left, tallest to the right, and where was the missus? Well, she was only down on her knees cleaning the en-suite toilet.

After three or so hours of this saga, starring Cathy the cleaner and Marion the house owner/employer, I decided to call a halt to the proceedings, but not before Cathy decided to steal my thunder.

'Harry?' called out my missus. 'That's Cathy finished. She'd like a lift home now!'

I was actually disappointed, because I was hoping she would say, 'Harry? That's Cathy starting, she'd like to know what to clean first!'

'Right, run her back home and give her £25, she did well,' the missus said, sounding convincing, but unaware that I had witnessed Cathy's cleaning within the house at first hand.

I was tempted to say, '£25? She did fuck all!'

However, I decided that this would be Cathy's severance pay included, and the sooner I dropped her off, the sooner I was rid of her!

I walked back into the house, prepared to lay down the law regarding Cathy's noticeable lack of elbow grease, but the missus was crashed out on the bed, totally exhausted and sleeping like a baby . . . I wonder why she was so tired?

As for Cathy, no doubt she was sitting in front of her TV thinking to herself, 'Not a bad day's work. Three hours away from the house, having been picked up and dropped off, with £25 cash in my pocket for allowing me the privilege to do so.'

Why can't I find a job like that?

I'm a Lesbian

...

I walked into a pub, sat down at the bar and ordered up a large whisky from the barman.

As I sat there sipping on it, a lovely young woman came over and sat down on a stool beside me.

'I'm sure I've seen you before, you're a policeman, aren't you?' she asked me.

I replied, 'Well, I've spent twenty-six years up to now serving in the police force, preventing crime, locking up neds, protecting property and serving the members of the public, so the answer to your question is yes, I'm a policeman!'

She smiled and nodded her head at me in acknowledgement.

'Well I'm a lesbian!' she said. 'I seem to spend my entire working day thinking about women.

'When I shower in the morning, I think of women.

'When I watch TV at night, I think of women. In fact, everything I seem to do makes me think of women, women, women!'

A few minutes later, a woman entered the bar and she excused herself and went over to talk with her.

Just at that, a man moved from the opposite end of the bar and came over and sat down beside me.

'I overheard part of your conversation there with the young lady. So, you're a real policeman then?' he asked.

To which I replied, 'Well, up until tonight I thought I was, but I've just found out that I'm a lesbian!'

Purl One

. . .

Safety campaigners are using snapshots of a female motorist pulling a jumper over her head whilst driving along a busy road in excess of 30 mph, to warn other drivers of the dangers.

The driver has since been given three penalty points and given a £30 fine for failing to be in proper control of her vehicle.

'It defies belief that anyone would think that is a smart thing to do!' said a spokesman from the road safety charity Safe Speed of Life.

At one stage, while having no eyes on the road, and no hands on the steering wheel, she was being totally disrespectful to other road users!

The incident took place on a road in Greenock, with the female driver at one stage having the jumper covering her full face and both her hands, with it above her head.

'Less than five yards ahead was a convoy of cars and lorries travelling along one of Inverclyde's busiest roads,' the spokesman added.

'If the car in front had braked even slightly, a serious or even fatal collision would have been unavoidable, due to her careless and inexcusable behaviour on the road.'

Apparently at one point, a police motorcyclist pursued her and drew up alongside, and was shouting at her, 'Pull-over! Pull-over!'

Whereby she screamed back at him, 'Naw, ya plonker! It's a JUMPER!'

Once again, the MENstruation period for a woman was

blamed in court for her totally out of character behaviour and subsequent outburst!

We men get the blame for everything ... The MENopause, the MENstrual cycle, the MENtal abuse, and MENingitis!

What Drugs?

* * *

A young drug dealer, who resided with his grandmother, was rummaging about in his room one day.

'Gran! Did you see a bottle of my tablets with LSD marked on the label?'

To which his frail old grandmother replied, 'Fuck your tablets! Have you seen the size of the dragons in that kitchen?'

The Racial Card

...

I was in the police station performing desk duties and reading through the Daily Briefing Register, when I came across several complaints regarding a florist in the area who had repeatedly been warned about parking his vehicles on the double yellow lines at the corner of the main street and causing great difficulty for public transport turning onto the street.

Steven, a young black officer on my shift, was working on the main street and was assigned to deal with the complaint, having been one of the officers who had issued him with a warning.

Armed with his fixed penalty notice book, Steven left the office to deal with the matter.

About an hour later, the door to the office opened and in walked a rather irate male florist.

'I want to register a complaint about one of your police officers,' he said rather indignantly.

'Okay sir,' I politely responded. 'And what would your complaint be?'

'I want to complain about him giving me parking tickets on my vehicles parked outside my shop!'

'Were your vehicles parked illegally?' I asked him.

'I don't think so, I own a shop there,' he replied.

'Well, who is the officer you wish to complain about?' I enquired, knowing fine well it was Steven.

'The policeman on the main street,' he said.

'Do you know his name or have his shoulder number?' I asked.

'I've left the parking tickets in the shop, but you must know him, he's been about the main street all week!'

Now at this point, he doesn't want to mention the fact that Steven is black. So I decided to tease him a little, to see how far he would go before he had to say.

'So it was the officer on the main street, you say?'

'Yes, it was him!'

'But you don't know his name or number?' I repeated.

'No I don't! But he's on the main street right now, booking the rest of my vehicles,' he replied.

'Okay, sir!' I said, slightly changing my direction. 'Well can you describe him for me – you know, his height, is he fat, thin, hair colour, wearing glasses, does he have a moustache? You know what I mean; anything that would help me to identify the officer?'

The florist was now beginning to squirm and feel a tad uneasy. Then out of the side of his mouth he mumbled, 'He's black!'

'Sorry, sir. Did you say he's back? I didn't quite hear you.'

'No! I said he's black,' he said louder, but more muffled.

'I'm so sorry, sir, but I'm not hearing what you are saying. Can you repeat that for me?' I asked, as he squirmed even more.

Suddenly he composed himself, looked at me straight on, face to face, and blurted out, loud and clear, 'He's black!' He then paused for a moment before continuing. 'It's that big black cop!'

I allowed my mouth to drop open, creating a look of total shock and surprise at his outburst, pausing only long enough to be nominated for a BAFTA award for my acting performance.

'Excuse me, sir, but are you complaining about him being black? I mean, I'd hate to think you were picking on this officer because of his skin colour.'

'Certainly not. I've nothing against his skin colour,' he said.

But I continued in this vein. 'I mean to say. It would not be the first time I've received malicious complaints, basically because of his colour.'

'Not at all! In fact . . .'

I interrupted as he was about to explain. 'Please tell me you're not a racist. Please! Are you, sir?'

He looked at me for a moment, digesting my question, then said, 'Tell you what, Officer, I think I'll just forget about the entire incident. It was only a couple of poxy parking tickets!'

At that he turned around and made for the office door.

I called after him. 'But your complaint, sir! What about your complaint?'

'Forget it!' he replied, slamming the office door shut as he left.

I just love my job.

Serving the members of the public and going out of my way to find an amicable solution to all their complaints!

Using the odd bit of 'black male' along the way!

P. T. E.

...

One Sunday morning, a police officer was on uniform mobile patrol duty, checking out the area for any stolen cars, abandoned from the previous night.

As he drove along a stretch of derelict road, he came across two people acting suspiciously in the bus shelter.

Due to the fact that the Sunday morning bus service would not start for another two hours, he decided he should pull over and check them out.

However, as he drew closer to the shelter he realised that it was a male and female, and they were oblivious to his arrival, due to being totally engrossed in what can only be described as wild, passionate, sexual intercourse against the glass window of the shelter.

Such was the erotic intensity and total focus of their love-making that before the officer could alight from his police car, the bus shelter glass window suddenly shattered under their pressure and they both fell through it, out onto the roadway screaming with ecstasy . . .

Him with pain and her with a mixture of pleasure and pain!

An ambulance was summoned immediately and they were both conveyed to the local Accident and Emergency.

Their morning of Public Transport Eroticism resulted in her sustaining a fractured coccyx and him with two broken wrists and some minor lacerations from the bus-shelter glass.

Who said outdoor sex wasn't good fun?

Embarrassing First Dates

• • •

If you were unlucky enough not to see this on the *Tonight* Show, I hope you're sitting down comfortably and relaxed when you read this. It's probably one of the funniest 'First Date' stories you're ever likely to read.

We have all encountered a bad date in our time, but this takes the prize!

The American host Jay Leno went into the studio audience to find the most embarrassing first date that a woman had ever had.

The overall winner described her worst experience, and there was absolutely no question as to why she took away the first prize.

She described the scene: mid-winter . . . snowing heavily and quite cold . . . and the guy had taken her skiing in the mountains, just outside Salt Lake City, in Utah.

It was advertised as a day trip, with no overnight accommodation. After all, they were relative strangers and had never met before.

The outing was basically just a bit of fun and relatively uneventful until they had packed up and were heading for home later that afternoon.

As they made their way back down the mountain, she suddenly began to realise that she should not have drunk that extra latte.

They were about an hour away from anywhere with a rest room and in the middle of nowhere!

Her companion suggested that she try and hold on, which she did for quite a while.

Unfortunately for her, because of the heavy snow falling, making it slow going, there came a point where she had to tell him that if he didn't stop and let her go out to the side of the road, she might have an accident on the front seat of his car.

Typical gentleman, on hearing these words, he made an emergency stop to allow her to get out of the car. Fortunately, she was wearing her fancy American pants, so one yank and they were down and she started almost immediately.

However, due to the deep snow, she couldn't get a good footing, so she sat back, letting her butt rest against the rear bumper of the car to steady herself.

Her companion stood at the opposite side of the car looking out for other traffic and was indeed a real gentleman, as he refrained from having a peek!

All she could think about was the relief she felt, despite the rather embarrassing situation she now found herself in.

Upon finishing, however, she soon became aware of another sensation as she tried to pull up her pants.

Due to the heat from her body against the freezing cold car, her buttocks were stuck solidly against the bumper.

Thoughts of tongues frozen to poles immediately crossed her mind as she attempted to disengage her flesh from the icy metal. It quickly became apparent that she had encountered a brand new problem, due to the extreme cold.

Horrified by her plight, but aware of the humour of the moment, she answered her date's concern about why it was taking so long, with the reply that she was 'freezing her butt off' literally, and was in need of some urgent assistance.

He walked around to her side of the car as she tried to cover up her modesty with her sweater and then she looked imploringly into his eyes and he burst out laughing!

She too had a fit of the giggles and when they finally managed to compose themselves, they assessed her latest dilemma.

As hysterical as the situation was, they were also faced with a serious problem, which they both agreed would require something hot to free her frozen cheeks from the grip of the metal.

Thinking about what had occurred in order to get her into this predicament in the first place, they both quickly realised that there was only one way to free her . . .

Drastic times call for drastic measures!

So, as she looked the other way, her first date proceeded to unzip his trousers, whip out his manhood and pee over her butt, to thaw her out and free her from the frozen bumper.

As the audience howled with laughter, she was presented with the *Tonight Show* prize, hands down.

Perhaps that should read 'pants down'!

So there you go – and you thought your first date was embarrassing?

Jay Leno's comment: 'This gives a whole new meaning to being totally pissed off!'

And lastly, how did her first date turn out?

He became her husband and was sitting alongside her in the audience!

Harry's Polis Contacts Page

• • •

Respectable Glasgow lawyer, 40 years old, seeks police-woman for live-in friendship, perhaps more. Duties will include cooking, typing, cleaning and accompanying me to office social functions. Must be prepared to study for law degree, willing to drop her briefs at a moment's notice, and take up soliciting as a full time career.
Police Box 15/20

Foreign to Me

...

I heard this story a long time ago and it still makes me laugh.

Two female traffic officers were patrolling the M8 motorway when they observed a vehicle in front being driven erratically from lane to lane.

Therefore the police officers decided to stop the vehicle and check the driver out.

The driver of the car immediately obeyed the signal to pull over and stop, where he then climbed out and walked back to the traffic car to speak with the officers.

The officers spoke with the male, who turned out to be a foreign visitor, who appeared none too steady on his feet and had to hold on to the police car for support.

The foreign male was displaying all the classic signs of being under the influence of alcohol.

After a few minutes, they were joined by the passenger of the car, who also appeared under the influence, but remained very quiet throughout the proceedings.

The roadside procedure of a breath test sample proved to be positive and, taking hold of the driver, they informed him that he was now under arrest.

It was only after the caution was administered that the driver asked in his broken English, 'It is customary in this country to give the breath test to the passenger, yes?'

As soon as he finished uttering this comment, the police officers looked over at his vehicle, which was foreign, with the steering wheel situated on the left-hand side, so the person whom they thought was the driver, was actually the passenger in the car.

Fortunately, it wasn't too late for them to rectify their mistake and duly arrest the real driver of the vehicle, who was standing alongside them watching the entire proceedings develop!

Hungry or What?

• • •

Another sign I saw recently was a large poster board outside an Indian restaurant, which read:

'TRY OUR CURRIES, YOU WON'T GET BETTER!'

Well I'm afraid with adverts like that outside your shop, 'NO ONE WILL TRY THEM, SO YOU WON'T GET ANY BUSINESS!'

Who's Laughing Now?

. . .

A convicted sex offender escaped from prison and broke into a house, where he tied up the young couple who lived in it.

He then leaned over the female and appeared to be kissing her neck and saying something.

When the convict eventually stopped and left them alone in a room while he went off to look for something to eat and drink, the husband leaned over and whispered to her.

'Darling, I heard about this guy in the news. He's a sex offender and he hasn't been with a woman for years.

'Don't try to resist him. Just co-operate fully with whatever he wants you to do, and if it's sexual intercourse, just do it and pretend you are really enjoying it – you don't want to upset him!'

Then he added, 'Just remember, it won't make a difference to our relationship. I'll always love you!'

His wife gave him a loving look and beckoned him to come closer to her, so she could whisper to him.

'Darling, I'm so relieved you feel that way, because he just told me that he was gay, he thinks you're really cute, and asked where do we keep the Vaseline.'

Then she added, 'So don't try to resist him. Just co-operate fully with whatever he wants you to do, and if it's sexual intercourse, just do it and pretend you are really enjoying it, you don't want to upset him!

'Oh, and darling, just remember this: I'll always love you too!

'But after tonight . . . You're on your own, gay boy!'

Go Before You Go-Go!

· · ·

Sometime back in 1997, two Greenock colleagues were instructed to attend at Inverness Police Headquarters to uplift a male being detained in custody, who was wanted on warrant.

It was about 11.30 pm when they set off in an unmarked CID police vehicle.

Now it just so happened that at this particular time the Hale-Bopp Comet could be clearly seen in the sky, and they seemed to be following it all the way to Inverness.

After a few hours of driving, the police passenger was desperate for a pee and asked his partner to pull over at the next parking area.

A few miles further along the A9 Perth road, they pulled in and stopped, and the desperate cop jumped out of the car and disappeared round the back of it.

The sky was pitch black, with only the moon, stars and comet clearly visible.

The police driver was so enthralled by the comet that he didn't take any notice of how long his partner had been away. However, a short while later he returned, cursing and swearing at his partner for not being the least bit concerned about his whereabouts, or the length of time it had taking him to return.

It appears that the time lapse was due to him standing relieving himself at the rear of the police vehicle, whilst also staring up at the moon and stars, but as he did this, he took one step backwards, lost his footing and slipped down the wet embankment into a muddy wet ditch at the bottom.

He stood there at the passenger door with his trousers covered in mud and his shoes and socks soaked right through.

You would think seeing this pitiful sight before him would conjure up some sympathy from his partner. Not a chance!

His partner immediately burst out laughing.

After the laughter died down, and with still some distance to travel, it was suggested that he take his shoes and socks off, put his shoes on the dashboard of the car for heat and hang the socks out of the window, jammed, to allow the rush of air as they drove along to help dry them off.

This done, they continued on their journey, but by the time they had reached their destination, his ankle socks had stretched and now resembled a black pair of nurse's nylon stockings! They were also still wet, and his shoes had dried to a light brown colour, due to the covering of mud on them.

This evoked more laughter from his unsympathetic partner.

As they entered the police station, the driver felt it was his duty to reassure the custody sergeant that he had not picked up a hobo on his way up, and after relaying the story to them, more laughter ensued. The description of events did not prevent them from having to endure some strange looks from their fellow officers in Inverness.

Fed and watered, cleaned and polished, they collected

their prisoner for escort and made their way back down the A9, without any enforced stops, arriving back at their station before their shift finished.

As you can imagine, there was quite a lot of banter among the shift on hearing what had taken place, but it was taken with good humour – well, what else could he do?

The moral of the story: Go, before you go-go, and you'll avoid any mishaps!

Good News, Bad News

• • •

A solicitor met with his ned client and said, 'The blood results are back and we have good news and bad news.'

'Give me the bad news first,' said the ned.

'Your DNA matches the blood found on the deceased, the murder weapon and the victim's car!'

'So what's the good news then?' the ned asked.

To which his solicitor replied, 'Your cholesterol levels are normal!'

Things Go Better With?

...

A well known fizzy drinks company announced today that we will soon be available to buy Viagra over the counter in liquid form, for the first time.

Apparently, Coca-Cola will market it as a power boosting beverage, suitable to be used as a mixer.

It will now be possible for a man, or woman, literally to pour themselves a 'stiff one'!

However, it's obvious that we can no longer refer to this as a 'soft drink', and it now gives new meaning to drink names such as 'Cocktails' and 'Highballs', never mind the reference to a good old-fashioned 'stiff drink'!

They are preparing to market their new concoction with their latest advertising campaign slogan:

'If whisky makes you frisky and brandy makes you randy, then one straight Coke will make you pregnant!'

Something to think about.

There is more money being spent on breast implants and Viagra today than on Alzheimer's research!

The British Medical Association is concerned that by the year 2040 there could be a large elderly population of women with perky boobs and men with huge erections, who have absolutely no recollection of what to do with them!

Pharmaceutical companies have submitted the latest examples of new generic names for Viagra, to be considered by a team of experts , but it appears they have already decided on Mycoxafloppin.

They state that careful consideration was given to

others, such as Mycoxafailin, Mydixadrupin, Mydixarizin and Dixafix.

All side effects will be dealt with by a highly effective course of Ibepokin!

Whatever Next?

· · ·

Is it just me? There I was driving down the road when I came across a big yellow police sign at the side of the kerb, with big bold letters declaring:

'POLICE NOTICE! ACCIDENT HERE ON TUESDAY NIGHT AT 7.30PM. WITNESSES WANTED!'

So, being an upholding member of the public and a former police officer, I made my way down there to witness this accident, which was apparently going to take place at 7.30 pm.

I should have known, after being there for approximately twenty minutes and nobody else had shown up, that the police had probably decided to cancel it without telling anybody!

However, it did strike me that things must be pretty bad in the police nowadays, when they have to advertise to get a decent road accident!

Brimstone and Fire!

...

Apart from being one of the senior members of the motorcycle section, Jimmy Lynch was also the motorcycle riding instructor.

Jimmy was a nice guy sometimes, but most of the time he was a cantankerous old bugger.

During my time in the section we had a motorcycle display team, where we did some fancy cross-over riding at speed and a variety of other daredevil tricks.

These were performed at festivals, fetes and the occasional international police tattoo.

On one particular occasion, Kenny Malcolm, having formed a good relationship with other bike-minded organisations, was asked if we would like to attend the military base in Catterick at the invitation of the White Helmet motorcycle display team, and train with them over the weekend.

As this was a good chance to work closely with a team of professionals, the entire police display team accepted the invitation gladly.

All equipped for the journey, we left in convoy for Catterick.

Whilst there, we watched with interest as the Helmets demonstrated their entire repertoire of tricks, which were impressive to say the least, carrying out their manoeuvres at breakneck speed and with inch perfection on their passing moves, narrowly avoiding a collision with each other by a hair's breadth.

Near the end of their display, they performed a stunt

called the Hoop of Fire, where the rider goes up a ramp at speed, takes off into the air and goes through a circle of fire, landing 'safely' on the opposite side, where the rider then does a lap of honour, acknowledging the applause of the spectators.

Now Jimmy was performing this stunt during our displays, but the White Helmets carried it out more spectacularly, using more bales of hay and more petrol, creating more fire and higher flames for a greater impact.

As it turned out, not long after this weekend visit, we had a motorcycle display to perform and, to add even more spice, Jimmy decided he would perform his daredevil Hoop of Fire stunt, the White Helmet way.

The extra bale of hay was added, raising the hoop higher and so the ramp for take-off also had to be raised to compensate.

Jimmy was really going for it this time and requested the extra fuel be used to soak the extra bale.

The display was going well with not one mistake or near miss during the entire show. And so it came down to the big finale, where Jimmy would perform his motorcycle jump through the Hoop of Fire!

The bales were lit and the flames soared high as Jimmy began his ascent up the ramp for take-off.

Whoosh! It appeared to have been executed to perfection, as Jimmy landed perfectly at the other side.

However, there was no lap of honour to accept the applause of a very enthusiastic crowd, as Jimmy came to a halt, dismounted his bike and ran over to a police traffic car, which immediately sped off . . . to the nearest hospital.

Jimmy had made the mistake of wearing his display team open-faced helmet and, as a result of the fierce, high flames, he had received severe burns to his face.

He was also missing eyebrows, eye lashes and his rather dapper moustache!

It was a few months after his recovery before Jimmy was able to return to duty, but when he did, there was the usual cruel banter, and signs stating 'Would Jimmy Lynch kindly extinguish himself before entering the motorcycle garage!'

Another trick was to stack several tins of haggis on his locker.

'What's this for?' Jimmy asked.

'This is just to let you know you're in the 'Burns section!' was the cruel reply.

Extremely Violent

· · ·

Police Headquarters were recently contacted by the area Mental Health Team and asked to assist in the execution of an arrest warrant for an extremely violent and dangerous mental health patient, residing at a local address within their area.

With a due sense of gravity appropriate to the situation, the officers taking part in the operation assembled in full uniform to enter the address, by force if need be, to make the arrest.

A procession of officers made their way along the street to the house, where entry was gained by force, in a professional manner, as the officers sprang into action, ready to subdue the suspect, who was described as an enraged giant of a man, who was ready to do them harm.

Unfortunately, he was out!

After several minutes of indecision within the house, they were alerted by a knock at the door, and they were informed by the next-door neighbour that the man they were looking for was outside in the street, approaching the house on foot.

The police team immediately scrambled and sprang into action for the second time in as many minutes, as they burst through the door onto the street outside, ready to meet this giant of a man with the fearsome reputation – but surprise, surprise! The great hulk they were expecting to confront turned out to be a quiet, sixty-year-old, frail old man measuring 4' 1" in height with his shoes on.

His reputation had been slightly exaggerated, to say the least.

It was left to one of the youngest officers in the team to approach him, with care, and ask, 'Will you come with us, please?'

To which he replied, without the slightest hesitation or physical resistance, 'Okay, sir!'

Situation dealt with, all the officers, attired in their special PSU kit, had the distinction of having to troop back along the street with their little frail, elderly male in custody and scores of residents looking on!

History's Most Original Contraceptives

...

Sixteen tadpoles fried in quicksilver, to be swallowed quickly by the woman immediately after intercourse. (Ancient China)

Let me answer on behalf of the ladies with twelve letters, nine of which are consonants and three vowels, all made up into three words:

'Fuck right off!'!

True Facts

• • •

Ghengis Khan killed his own brother over an argument about fish! Apparently he didn't ask for salt and vinegar on his.

Thirty-one-year-old Brenda Hunter, of Illinois, shot her brother in 1994 because she disliked the type of cheese he put on her chilli dinner! Hmm! Where did he get it from?

Peter Weiller, a German film buff, was beaten to death by the cinema ushers in 1994 because he had brought his own popcorn! In his defence, he did pay for his Coke.

A Frenchman called Noel Carriou killed both of his wives because they were poor cooks. As a result, he was sentenced to eight years in jail in 1978 after he killed his second wife for cooking him an overdone roast. Seventeen years earlier, he had broken his first wife's neck after she too served him an overcooked meal. In sentencing him, the judge sympathised with Carriou and stated, 'Good cooking is an important part of married life!' If that was the case, owners of chip shops would be getting murdered every day in Glesca.

Heinrich Gembach of Munich choked his wife to death in 1995, by force-feeding her wheat cereal. He told the police that this was what he'd had for breakfast every morning for the last ten years! The only problem was, he put out his own breakfast every morning, so the judge sentenced him to life, because he regarded him as a cereal killer.

Restaurant owner Gilbert Menezes was sent for trial in 1996 for killing his wife's lover, then serving his liver with fried onions to his customers! Nothing up with that if it's cooked properly – after all, liver is very good for you.

What a Liar
· · ·

Tommy was in court charged with a double murder.

The judge said, 'You are charged with beating your wife to death with a hammer.'

A man at the rear of the court shouted out, 'You bastard!'

The judge ignored his outburst and continued.

'You are also charged with beating your wife's lover to death with a hammer.'

The man at the rear of the court shouted out again, 'You dirty rotten bastard!'

This time the judge looked at the man and said, 'Sir, I can understand your anger at this crime, but I will not tolerate any more outbursts. If you have anything to say, then say it now!'

At that, the man at the rear of the court got to his feet and said, 'For fifteen years I lived next door to that bastard. And every time I asked to borrow a bloody hammer, the bastard said he didn't have one!'

Scottish Book Trust

•••

As an author, I am extremely fortunate and privileged to be registered with the Scottish Book Trust, to perform live literature events.

This privilege allows me, as an author and storyteller, to be invited to visit areas around Scotland that I would never have the opportunity to appear in, simply because of the expense involved and the attending audiences available.

I myself have performed my 'Stand-Up Storytelling' to an audience of only five people before, and on another occasion four hundred, such is the difference in the turn out from area to area.

However, one particular booking I received was for an author event in Dornoch up in the north-west Highlands.

After driving for almost the entire day, I finally reached my destination and called my contact for directions to the location of the event.

The event was being held in a small community hall and after a quick something to eat and a change into my author gear, I arrived promptly at the hall, which was set up with rows of chairs in front of the stage, to meet with the organiser.

The starting time of the event came . . . and went, as we both waited patiently for the audience to turn up.

Sadly, after about forty minutes, we were still there, together – and alone! So I came up with a suggestion.

'Look, mate! It doesn't appear to have been very well advertised, and I can't see anybody attending now, so what do you say we both head for the nearest pub and I'll tell you some of my stories over a cool beer?'

'Okay!' he said. 'But I'll be about twenty minutes.'

'Twenty minutes? How come?' I asked him.

To which he replied rather dejectedly, 'Because some daft bugger's got to put all the chairs back!'

That's a Charity
• • •

A driver is stuck in a traffic jam.

As he looks out of his car window, he sees a boy on a skateboard weaving his way through the traffic towards him.

'Hey, son, what's the hold up?' he asks.

'It's some bammy lawyer,' the boy replies.

'Apparently he's got money problems. So he's doused himself with petrol and is lying in the middle of the road threatening to set fire to himself. We're taking up a collection for him.'

'How much have you got so far?' the driver asks.

The boy replies, 'About fourteen gas lighters and three gallons of petrol!'

Cursing on the Course

· · ·

Big Donnie Henderson was disqualified from the police divisional golf tournament for foul and abusive language. As a result he was charged with bringing the force into disrepute and had to report to the Chief Constable to be disciplined.

'So, Constable Henderson, when exactly did you use this disgraceful language?' the Chief asked.

'Last week, sir, while I was competing in the force divisional golf tournament. I had just hit one of the best tee shots of my entire career, but my golf ball hit an overhead electrical power line and plummeted to the ground, having travelled only about fifty yards.'

'Is that when you swore?'

'No, sir!' Donnie replied. 'After it hit the ground, a dog ran out from some nearby bushes, grabbed my ball in his mouth and ran off with it!'

'Is that when you swore and became abusive?' the Chief asked again.

'Not exactly, sir,' Donnie said. 'Just at that moment, an eagle appeared in the sky, flew down and grabbed the dog in its claws and flew off with it.'

'So is that when you swore?' asked the astonished Chief.

'No, not yet,' Donnie replied. 'As the eagle flew off with the dog, it headed towards the green, and just as it passed over a clump of trees next to the green, the dog dropped my ball.'

'Did you swear then?' the Chief asked, becoming exasperated.

'No!' Donnie said. 'Because just at that minute, the ball struck a tree, careered off a large rock, bounced over a sand bunker onto the green, and stopped within six inches of the hole.'

To which the Chief responded, 'Oh! Don't tell me you missed the fucking putt?'

Trust in Jesus!

· · ·

A housebreaker is stealing from a house when he hears a voice say, 'Jesus is watching you!'

To his relief, he turns around to see a parrot looking on.

'What's your name?' he asks.

The parrot replies, 'Moses.'

'Moses?' the housebreaker repeats. 'What sort of person calls their parrot Moses?'

To which the parrot replies, 'The same sort of person who calls that big fierce Rottweiler behind you Jesus!'

Ice Cold Moggy

• • •

One Sunday morning, local cop Dick Waddell was on mobile patrol, checking for stolen vehicles in the Craigmillar area of Edinburgh, commonly referred to as the jungle.

The area was a regular dumping ground for joy riders to abandon the stolen cars after they were finished.

Dick stopped in front of a car with a door open and, after making a routine check, it was confirmed by his controller that he had recovered a stolen car and they were arranging a breakdown truck to attend and remove it to the police pound.

While awaiting the arrival of the breakdown truck, he heard shouting and swearing coming from the nearby tenement close.

Dick was just getting out of his panda car to check where it was coming from, when suddenly clothes, books, ornaments, plates and shoes were thrown from the second-floor veranda.

This resembled a scene from the former TV game show *Don't Forget Your Toothbrush*, where household items were chucked out the windows and doors into the garden.

He attended at the house regarding the disturbance and the door was opened by a big crabbit-looking female, who in her eloquent Craigmillar accent, politely enquired of Dick, 'Whit the fuck dae you want, Cluedo?'

Dick's response was immediately to warn her about her conduct, coupled with the disturbance she was causing and the dangers of throwing objects over the veranda.

To which the big female replied, 'Well that's nothing! If ye had waited for another five minutes afore coming tae the door, that wee bastard in there would have been the next tae go!' She was referring to her boyfriend.

It transpired that the boyfriend, who was a scrawny wee runt, had been cheating with the next-door neighbour and had been caught out.

To make matters worse, Dick warned them that if he had to return due to them fighting and causing a disturbance, he would arrest them both for breach of the peace.

At that, he left the house to return to the abandoned stolen car at the front of the tenement, when he heard an almighty crash coming from outside on the street.

Thinking that someone had collided with the stolen car, he ran down the stairs and, as he looked outside, he saw the breakdown truck driver looking up at the building.

When Dick looked over at his police panda car, he realised what the crashing sound had been, for embedded in the roof of his car was a fridge, with the contents scattered over the bonnet.

A police van was summoned to attend at the locus, where the big female and her scrawny boyfriend were apprehended for breach of the peace and malicious mischief.

As for the police panda, it was carted off along with the stolen car and, as a result of the damage caused by the fridge on the roof, it was subsequently written off.

Because fridges are better when kept in the kitchen!

Doing Good Business!

...

Two young entrepreneur businessmen in London were sitting down for a break in their soon to be opened shopping store.

As yet the store had only a few shelves and rails fixed to the walls.

As they sat there savouring a cup of coffee, one said to the other, 'I'll bet you any minute now some thick tourist is going to walk by, look in the window, then open the door and ask what we're selling.'

As soon as the words were out of his mouth, sure enough, a curious Scotsman looked in the window, then opened the door and in a broad Scottish accent asked, 'What are you selling in here?'

One of the businessmen replied sarcastically, 'We're selling arseholes!'

Quick as a flash the Scotsman replied, 'Business must be doing very well . . . Only two left?'

Englishmen, God bless them, they just shouldn't mess with a Scotsman!

Mistaken Identity

・・・

Two detective officers were investigating a complaint regarding a minor assault and attended at the house of a young mother.

As they were invited inside the house, they noticed the grandmother was also present, but there was no sign of the child's father.

While the mother went off to the kitchen to make some tea, the detective sergeant decided to exercise the full extent of his people skills and entered into some small talk with the grandmother in the lounge.

'That's a nice photo of your grand-daughter on the mantelpiece behind you,' he said.

'Thank you!' she replied.

He then lifted the photograph up to look at it more closely.

'I take it that must be your son-in-law holding the baby in that photograph there. He's a big fella, isn't he?'

The grandmother slowly turned her head to look, and taking the photograph from his hand, she replied, 'No, Detective Sergeant, he isn't, that's me!'

The young detective constable accompanying him was sworn to secrecy regarding the incident, and in true police fashion, he told everyone and anyone!

Penny For Your Thoughts

· · ·

Two men are driving through Glasgow when they get stopped by a motorcycle cop for speeding.

The driver rolls down his window as the cop approaches his side of the car. Suddenly the cop wallops him across the head with his torch.

'Ouch! What was that for?' the driver asks, rubbing his head.

The motorcycle cop says, 'In Glasgow, we expect drivers to produce their driving licence to us when we approach their window.'

The cop then issues him with a speeding ticket.

Just as the driver is about to roll up his window, the cop hits him over the head again.

'Ouch! What the hell was that for this time?' he asks.

'In Glasgow when we issue you with a ticket, we expect you to be polite and say thank you!' the cop replies.

The driver duly obeys and thanks the motorcycle cop for issuing him with the speeding ticket, before quickly rolling up his window.

The motorcycle cop then walks around to the passenger side and knocks on the window.

As the passenger rolls down his window, the cop wallops him across the head with his baton.

'Ouch!' the passenger yells with the pain and says, 'What the hell did you do that for?'

'I was making your wish come true!' the cop says.

'What fucking wish?' the passenger asks.

'The one that you would have had fifty metres down the

road, when you would have turned to your pal and said, "I wish that big bastard had tried that shit with me!"'

That's Okay!
• • •

My next-door neighbour was driving his daughter to school, when he inadvertently turned right at a 'No Right Turn' sign.

'Shit! I just made an illegal turn,' he said.

'Don't worry about it, Dad!' replied his daughter. 'The police car behind us did the exact same thing!'

Order of the Court
• • •

True Stories from the Law Courts:

PROCURATOR FISCAL: Is your appearance here in court this morning pursuant to a deposition notice, which my office sent to your solicitor?

WITNESS: No, this is how I always dress when I go to work.

The Secrecy Button

· · ·

During my time working at Craigie Street, we had an enquiry department who dealt with all public sudden deaths.

A call would be received regarding a member of the public whose next of kin had been found within a house or had collapsed in the street and, as a result, had subsequently died.

The officer attending the incident would obtain all details pertaining to the deceased and their relatives.

If no death certificate was issued by their own GP then a post-mortem would be carried out to determine the cause of death.

Thereafter, if no suspicious circumstances were found, a report would be issued, along with the death certificate.

The inquiry department, or the officer dealing with the family, would contact them to call and uplift the certificate and the necessary funeral arrangements would then be made.

This particular death involved an elderly Irishman and as per procedure his next of kin had been traced to Ireland and informed to attend.

About seven of the family called the police station several times, and spoke with several of the inquiry team, who had difficulty understanding them, due to them talking fast, with unusual pikey accents, and celebrating his passing with a wake. However, due to a delay, they were asked to call back.

Later that day they called and the officer answering the

telephone instantly recognised who it was. 'Hold on a minute and I'll put you through to the officer dealing with it.'

At that, he double-clicked the secrecy button – in effect, putting the phone on mute – but accidentally switched it off again and, not realising his mistake, he held the phone up and shouted out across the busy room.

'Donald! It's for you. It's one of those drunken gadgie mob from Ireland on the phone about their uncle!'

Everyone in the office focussed on the telephone and cringed!

The Disturbance

· · ·

Two cops attend a complaint regarding a disturbance coming from a tenement close house at three o'clock in the morning.

After gaining entry to the house, they discover the householder playing loud music, singing and dancing.

They arrest the male involved and he appears next morning at the court.

The Sheriff asks him how he pleads to the charge of breach of the peace.

'Guilty, m'lord, wi' mitigating circumstances!' he replies.

'What mitigating circumstances?' asks the Sheriff.

'Ah cannae sleep!'

'So what do you do all day?' the Sheriff asks.

'Well, I get up out of bed about nine o'clock and have a plate o' cornflakes, followed by a bottle of whisky as a chaser.

Then in the afternoon, I head for the pub for some lunch and have one, sometimes two bottles of wine. After which I head for the bookies for a wee flutter on the horses. Purely as a wee hobby and to give me something to think about.

'After the last race, I'll head for the chippie and get a fish supper for my tea, and usually wash it down with a bottle of malt whisky.

'Some nights, before the pub shuts, I'll nip down and have five or six pints of Guinness before I head for home.'

'Let me just add that up,' the Sheriff says. 'You have two

bottles of spirits, two bottles of wine and five or six pints of Guinness, and you say you can't sleep?'

'Correct!' the accused replies.

'How come?' the Sheriff asks.

To which the accused replies, 'Cause I'm usually awake all night singing and dancing!'

Carnival of Fun
• • •

A cop was on duty working at the carnival and he befriended one of the girls working there.

They both agreed that at the end of his shift they would go back to her caravan on the site.

As he entered her caravan, he was surprised by the amount of teddy bears and cuddly toys she had scattered around the room and on every work surface.

After a night of passion, the cop rolled over and asked her, 'So how did I do?'

To which the female replied, 'Help yourself to any prize on the bottom shelf!'

Old Bob MacDonald

. . .

Old Bob was another who joined the police after completing his service with the armed forces – in this case, the Royal Navy.

Fortunately, being ex-navy, he walked with a rolling gait, and coupled with the fact that he enjoyed a wee libation, on or off duty, day or night, this made his manner of walking the ideal cover for his liquid intake on many an occasion!

It was his partners who had to look out, as he bumped into them regularly while they walked alongside him on the street.

One nightshift, he was accompanied on the beat by a young probationer and, as was normal, the senior cop would show them the pubs – I mean the ropes!

Anyway, they stopped off at several licensed drinking establishments on his beat and felt obliged to sample their wares on offer.

Within a very short time, Bob was a wee bit under the weather. In other words, totally pished!

The young probationer Neil, with considerably more sense, decided he had better take Bob away, out of view of the public and the supervisors.

Neil guided Bob to the nearby Gorbals station – not a wise choice of venue.

On seeing Bob's condition, the duty sergeant instructed Neil to take Bob out of sight and sober him up!

Neil didn't have a lot of options open to him, so he took Bob into the shower room at the rear of the station.

He carefully helped Bob undress and led him into the shower, in an attempt to try and sober him up.

Bob was not for staying in, so Neil quickly stripped off too and went into the shower with him to prevent him from leaving.

Unfortunately, the patrol sergeant big Bob Maguire was on the look-out for old Bob, and somehow tracked them down to the shower room.

What a surprise for the sergeant when he entered the room, to find both beat cops in the shower together, one totally blootered and the other completely embarrassed and trying to rinse himself down the nearest drain.

As procedure demands, the duty inspector was summoned to attend the shower room.

Fortunately, he was very understanding and, despite protestations from the patrol sergeant, who wanted them sacked, the duty inspector instructed old Bob to be taken home to sober up.

As a result of this episode, old Bob was banished to Pollokshaws police office to work inside, where he ended his police service in quiet solitude – and reasonably sober!!

However, although rumours persisted about two naked police officers being found in the shower together, no mention was ever made about their identity . . . until now!

But the question has to be asked:

Why was the patrol sergeant more concerned about them having been drinking, and not the slightest bit bothered about them sharing the shower in their underwear?

Hospital Patter

• • •

Recently, my wife had to spend a few days in a Lanarkshire hospital and I went at visiting time to see her.

She was sharing a room with three other women and as I walked into the ward she was in conversation with the patient in the next bed, a young girl in her late twenties, with two older woman patients directly opposite on the other side of the room.

My wife immediately introduced me to the young woman, whose name was Casey from Easterhouse, in Glasgow.

I tried to make polite conversation.

'How come you're in this hospital?'

'I'm no' really sure. Ah think the ambulance driver got lost and just dropped me aff here. Coming fae Easterhouse, ah should be in the Royal!'

I then foolishly asked her what she was in the hospital with.

To which she explained in her broken English – or should I say, broad Glaswegian accent, 'The doctor said ah've got sumfin' wrang wi' ma pancreas. Ah don't know whit the medical term for it is, but basically it's fucked!'

Slightly surprised by her blunt, descriptive answer, I replied, 'Oh, right!'

At that, she looked over at one of the older ladies opposite, who was rubbing her nose frantically, and asked, 'Whit's up wi' yer nose, Aggie?'

The elderly female strained her face and replied, 'What?'

'Ah said, whit's up wi' yer nose? Ye're giving it pelters and rubbing it like mad.'

To which Aggie then replied, 'Oh, ah'm deaf, but it annoys me. Ah'm fed up telling them, I'm better without it, it's just a bloody nuisance!'

'Ye're deaf because yer nose annoys ye?' Casey asked.

Aggie looked straight at her, still making faces and straining to hear. 'Awe, bugger it, Casey, I'll need tae put it on again. Ah cannae make oot a word ye're saying, hen!' After much hassle trying to find it, she fitted her hearing aid onto her ear and said, 'Right, hen, whit were ye saying again?'

To which Casey said, 'Ah wis just wantin' tae know if my radio was up too loud for ye!'

This time Aggie replied, 'Ah still cannae hear ye right. It's that bloody radio of yours, it's up too loud. You're gonnae end up deaf!'

Casey then looked over at my wife and gave a wicked smile, before saying, 'Thank Christ you're here, Marion! It's been hellish. I've been desperate tae talk tae somebody normal! The only fun I've had was when Aggie was sleeping wi' her gub wide open and I was trying tae throw grapes in it tae waken her up.'

'Oh right!' my wife replied, before looking over at me, raising her eyebrows and whispering, 'Cancel the fruit!'

The Siamese Twins

• • •

Two Siamese twin brothers decided to take a trip to France.

Due to their physical condition, there was great interest in their arrival and as a result the media were never far away.

After a week, one of the big TV companies asked for an interview with them, to which they agreed.

'Do you come to France because of the wonderful cuisine?'

'No! We do not enjoy the food. It's minging!' they replied.

'Well, is it for our fine wines?' they were asked.

'No! The wine tastes like pure piss,' they said bluntly.

'Well! Is it the wonderful sights, like the Eiffel Tower?'

'No! That's just a pile of scrap metal,' was their response.

'Well, if you do not like our food, our wine and our wonderful sights, why do you come to France?' the TV interviewer asked.

To which one of them replied, 'It's the only time my brother gets a chance at the driving!'

Marriage Means Sharing

. . .

An elderly couple entered Burger King and sat down at a table. After a few minutes, the old man got up and walked over to the counter where he placed an order for a hamburger with French fries and a drink.

He then returned to the table where his wife was seated waiting for him and unwrapped the hamburger and carefully cut it in half, placing one half in front of his wife.

Next, he counted out the French fries, dividing them equally into two small piles and neatly placed one pile in front of his wife.

At that, he took a sip of the drink, then his wife took a sip, and placed the cup on the table between them.

The old man began to eat his half of the burger.

All the while, the people seated next to them were looking over and whispering.

Obviously they were thinking, 'That poor old couple, all they can afford is one meal between the two of them!'

As the old man finished his half of the hamburger, he began to eat his share of the French fries, when a young man came up to their table and politely offered to buy them another meal.

The old man replied that they were fine and that they were used to sharing everything.

Other diners closer to them noticed that the old lady hadn't eaten a bite. She just sat there watching her husband eat and occasionally took turns at sipping the drink.

Again the young man approached their table and

begged them to let him buy another meal for them, but the old lady answered, 'No thank you. We're used to sharing everything.'

Finally, as the old man finished and was wiping his face with the napkin, the young man approached for a third time, focusing on the old lady, who had yet to eat a single bite of food, and politely asked, 'What are you waiting for?'

The old lady looked at him and replied, 'THE TEETH!'

The Dawn Chorus

• • •

I was awakened early this morning. The earth lay cool and still.

Suddenly, a tiny little bird flew over, landing on my window sill.

It began to sing a song so lovely, so sweet and oh so gay.

Slowly, all my troubles, my aches and pains began to slip away.

He sang of far-off places, of laughter and lots of fun.

It seemed like his very chirping brought up the early-morning sun.

I stirred beneath the covers and slipped slowly out of my bed.

And gently shut the window down and crushed his fucking head . . .

Sorry, readers, but I'm just not a morning person!

The Notebook Diary

· · ·

PC & WPC Notebook Diary, page 1, a Saturday in November.

WPC: He was very quiet and subdued, definitely not himself. Something was wrong. He hadn't kissed me at all tonight.

Not even looked in my direction. I think he's seeing another policewoman.

I went to my bed and cried for hours! He eventually followed me upstairs later and cuddled me, while I stroked his hair.

He lay still for a while, before we made such wonderful and meaningful love and after it, we fell asleep in each other's arms.

PC: Scotland lost today, totally gutted . . . Got a ride though!

Foot 'n Mouth

· · ·

Several policewomen were out for a girlie night, accompanied by some of their close friends.

One of the women present just happened to be dating a well-known professional footballer.

During the evening, the girls were joined by four older men, who stated they were all involved in a dental practice.

The usual patter was spouted about having lovely teeth and that their dental practice was one of the more reputable ones.

However, the footballer's girlfriend intimated that she was looking for a good dentist to go to for some cosmetic work.

Quick as a flash, the elder of the four men thrust his hand out and put his finger in her mouth and began probing and pulling on her cheeks, to view her teeth.

Unfortunately, as he was behaving in this totally unprofessional manner, with his fingers in her mouth, her footballer boyfriend had entered the night club.

On seeing this disgusting act being performed on his girlfriend, who appeared disturbed and embarrassed by the entire episode, the footballer rushed over, knocked him to the floor and automatically kicked him full in the face!

The police were called and interviewed everyone involved in the incident, whereby the elder male explained that he was a dentist, hence the reason for putting his fingers in her mouth.

On hearing this excuse for his behaviour towards his girlfriend, the boyfriend stated that he was a professional footballer and had reacted, albeit accidentally, and kicked him in the head when he was on the floor, believing his head to be a ball!

After further enquiries, it transpired that the elder male and his party were all in fact private-hire taxi drivers on a night out, and apart from a cut lip and a few loose teeth, he did not wish to make any complaint.

Mind you, if you are going to go around putting your fingers into a complete stranger's mouth, it's a safe bet that you're going to require to see a dentist the following morning!

A bit of advice, my friend: it's much safer to be a taxi driver, and just drive them round the bend!

Speeding Kills

• • •

A farmer received a phone call from one of his farmhands, who blurted out excitedly, 'I've just run over a pig and it's stuck under the tractor!'

'Is it still alive?' the farmer asked.

'Aye! Still alive. What should I do?' he said, desperately seeking advice.

'Right! Just shoot it,' the farmer said. 'Then bury it in the field.'

Several minutes later the farmer gets another call from the farmhand.

'I've done that. Now what will I do with his fucking speed camera?'

It's A Miracle!

• • •

The police doctor had just finished his examination of a very attractive young policewoman and asked her, 'Are you married, PW Riley?'

'No, Doctor, I'm single. Why?' she replied.

'Well, have you been sleeping with your boyfriend, Miss Riley?'

'Oh no, Doctor. I don't have a boyfriend. I'm single and live alone!' she replied.

'Well have you been going out with other men on your shift and having a casual sexual relationship?' he asked.

'Certainly not, Doctor Campbell, such a thing would be unthinkable and totally out of character for me!' she responded.

'Are you sure about that, Miss Riley?' he said. 'Bearing in mind that I now have the results of the urine sample back from the lab, do you still say you've not had anything to do with any man?'

'I'm positive! I think I'd know about it if I did! Now may I leave?' responded a rather indignant Miss Riley.

'No!' the doctor replied abruptly.

'No? Why not?' she asked.

To which the police doctor replied sarcastically, 'Because, Miss Riley, at this particular point, I'm awaiting my secretary to ring me through and announce the arrival, in my surgery, of Three Wise Men bearing gifts!'

The Driving School

· · ·

All aspiring Jackie Stewarts and Jim Clarks in the police had to attend a two-week driving course in Glasgow, in order to be taught the system of driving and the theory test, and if you passed it, then you qualified as an expert police driver.

One of the cops on the course was Colin 'Gallus' Muir, so nicknamed because everything to him was a dawdle!

Part of the course was to show that you were proficient in the handling of various vehicles – the land rover, the divisional van and any saloon car being used as a panda.

Gallus was performing well, up until the manoeuvrability test, which consisted of a series of emergency stops, driving at speed through a slalom marked out with traffic cones and reversing the vehicle into a garage space, all within a certain time limit.

He drove the course like a seasoned expert, performing his emergency stops, weaving in and out between the cones and then reversing at speed into the garage well within the permitted time. Unfortunately, he forgot to stop in time, and collided with the six-foot-high brick wall at the rear of the garage space, causing extensive damage to the police car and demolishing the wall!

Such careless driving would normally result in an immediate return to beat duties, but after some serious discussion, where scratching of the heads took place, as well as other body parts, it was decided that Gallus had some potential, and therefore would be allowed to continue.

Gallus was not about to let this minor mishap hinder

him, and he carried on as before until the final day of his test drive.

As he drove along the road, displaying his expert driving skills to the traffic inspector seated beside him for the test, he was instructed, 'At the roundabout, go straight ahead.'

Obeying the instructions, Gallus, being Gallus, drove the police car straight over the roundabout, leaving deep tyre tracks on the grass and scattering flower heads and stems as he totally destroyed the decorative flower bed and focal point in the centre!

This was a complete disaster for the driving school test instructor and a manoeuvre that was totally unacceptable from a sober police driver.

This time there was no discussion about it as Gallus was sent back to his division to walk the beat in disgrace.

Fortunately for Gallus, he was highly regarded by some of the senior officers and, several months later, when all had died down and was back to normal, he was given a reprieve and allowed to return in order to re-sit his driving test.

This time, a wiser Gallus passed the course and final test with flying colours.

However, the embarrassment and humiliation he experienced after his roundabout incident continued to haunt him, and this was most notable when he was the driver and instructed to attend a call in another area of the division. It would take him double the time of another police driver to reach the location, due to Gallus looking for a suitable route that didn't include roundabouts!

I wonder why?

Get Off My Toe

• • •

Having followed the last few episodes of *Strictly Come Dancing*, I thought I would have a go at trying ballroom dancing myself.

I joined a local dance school who were advertising and went along for my first lesson.

The lady running the school spoke very Glaswegian and looked a real rough diamond who was not to be messed with.

During one disastrous attempt at a two-step, I accidentally trod on her toes, several times.

'I'm terribly sorry, but I'm a little stiff from badminton!' I said.

To which she quickly responded, 'And here I thought you were just another clumsy bastard from Glasgow!'

Off Your Head

• • •

A cop was on desk duty at Pollok police office one night when he received a call from a man who asked him, 'Has any of the mental patients escaped out of the Leverndale Hospital tonight?'

'Not that I'm aware of, sir!' the officer answered.

'Are you sure about that?' the caller asked.

'Why are you asking that?' the officer said.

To which he replied, 'Because some bampot has just ran off with my wife!'

Fact or Fiction?

. . .

Brief scenario as follows: Justin falls over during his school break and scrapes his knee. His teacher, Miss Brown, discovers him crying in the playground and gives him a cuddle to comfort him.

Back in the 1960s, Justin would soon feel better after his cuddle and return to the playground to continue having fun.

Present day, Miss Brown would be interviewed by the female and child unit of the police, accused of being a sexual predator, expelled from her position as a teacher and required to resign, stand trial at a court case and face the possibility of three years' imprisonment with her name added to the sexual offenders' file.

As for Justin, he has to endure five years of therapy, after which, a year later, he comes out of the closet and announces he is gay!

Fact or fiction?

Trouble Maker

...

On the day that a ned is released from prison for serious assault, after he beat up another male with whom he had been drinking earlier, he re-enters what was his local pub, before his conviction.

The inside has been altered and painted with bright, decorative colours and there is a more camp atmosphere about the place.

But he ignored the décor and sat down on a stool at the bar, where he ordered up his favourite drink: a double vodka and ice with a bottle of Stella Artois.

He sat there at the bar without talking to anyone, ordering up drink after drink.

After he had quickly consumed several drinks, the ned was becoming more and more aggressive as he perused his surroundings.

Suddenly, he climbed up onto the bar and announced to all, 'Every one of you sitting on the left-hand side of this pub is a pure wanker! Anybody want to disagree with me?'

Not one patron on the left side of the pub uttered a word or made the slightest of movements.

Disgusted with their lack of balls, the ned looked over at the other side of the pub and shouted, 'Every one of you sitting on the right side of the pub is an out and out poofter! Anybody want to disagree with me now?'

Not one person on the opposite side of the pub moved, apart from a little old man on the left side of the pub who stood up.

'Hey you!' shouted the ned. 'Are you looking for some trouble, wee man?'

'Definitely not!' replied the old man. 'It's just that I would appear to be sitting on the wrong side of the pub!'

The Chief Constable's Ball

• • •

This has absolutely nothing to do with tickets for a raffle!

A young police officer, who had recently completed the Accelerated Promotion Course, obtained a ticket to attend the Chief Constable's Ball.

Arriving late, he watched as everyone was up on the floor dancing, with the exception of one woman: the Chief Constable's wife.

Hoping to make an impression, he made his way towards her and politely introduced himself, before asking her, 'May I have the pleasure of your company on the dance floor, ma'am?'

The Chief's wife looked him up and down before replying rather rudely, 'I don't dance with a child!'

Quick as a flash the young officer responded, 'My sincere congratulations to you and the Chief Constable, ma'am, I would have thought you were both past the stage of having more children!'

He still looks back at his career and wonders where it all went wrong!

D.N.A. All the Way

...

A ned was apprehended as a suspect for a number of armed robberies around Scotland, whereby a knife had been used, and he was taken into custody.

After being interviewed for several hours by the C.I.D. officers from the area where he was arrested, they were getting nowhere, and so other officers arrived from another police force in order to interview him too.

As each question regarding the robberies was put to the suspect, he sat impassively throughout alongside his solicitor. On the solicitor's advice, he would only answer, 'No comment', to each and every one of their questions.

Finally, one of the C.I.D. officers got fed up and said to the suspect, 'Right, Mister "No comment"! I'm going to require a sample of your blood, a sample of your stool and a sample of your urine for D.N.A. analysis.'

The suspect immediately looked over at his solicitor and asked, 'How do they take that?'

The solicitor replied nonchalantly, 'Just give them your underpants!'

Whereabouts!

· · ·

After a terrorist bomb blast in the centre of London, the emergency services and rescue workers were combing through the rubble when they discovered a young girl covered in blood, but still alive.

'Where are you bleeding from?' asked the paramedic.

To which she replied in a broad Glaswegian accent, 'Govan! But whit the fuck has that got tae dae wi' you?'

So There!

· · ·

A woman was arguing with her housemaid, and before leaving the room the maid decided to give the woman a piece of her mind in return and tell her exactly what she thought.

'You might like to know that your husband regards me as a far better housekeeper and cook than you are. He also said I was much better looking!'

The woman remained silent while she continued to rant.

'That's not all,' the maid continued. 'I'm better than you in bed!'

'I suppose my husband told you that as well?' asked the woman.

The maid hesitated before replying, 'No. The gardener did!'

Have a Nice Day!

• • •

It was a warm summer afternoon and Ricky Day was patrolling the town centre.

As it was lunchtime, it was fairly quiet, with many of the shops closed.

Ricky stopped to chat to some old guys sitting by the decorative fountain in the town square and was remarking about how quiet and peaceful it was.

'Aye!' one of the old guys replied. 'The best time of the day, waiting for the bookies to open, although the way my luck has went recently picking horses, I'd be as well picking my nose – at least I'd see something for it!'

Ricky bade them farewell and sauntered up the road, where he saw a large van parked on the double yellow lines on the road outside the electrical retailer's shop. As he stopped to check it, a man came out of the shop, staggering under the weight of a large television.

The man blamed the manager for having to park at the front of the shop, and not at the rear loading bay. The manager had forgotten to leave the keys for the back door, and it was only because they had urgent deliveries to do that they used the front.

As a result, he gave them permission to carry on, and was assured by the man that they only had another six TVs to load, and they would be on their way.

He then thanked Ricky and instructed him to, 'Have a nice day, Officer!'

Ricky carried on with his beat and later made his way back to the police station to go off duty.

He was only in the office for about ten minutes when the Inspector came through and enquired as to who had been patrolling the town centre that day.

'That was me, Inspector,' he replied.

'Did you pass the big electrical shop in the High Street at lunchtime?' he asked.

'Yes, sir!' Ricky innocently replied.

'Well the fucking place was broken into during their dinner hour and the bastards are away with about twenty TVs and umpteen other electrical items!'

Ricky immediately told him about the man who had been loading the van outside the front of the shop, and the fact that he had stopped and spoken with him.

The Inspector almost burst a blood vessel at this news.

'You're telling me you had a wee blether with these guys, while they were stealing twenty fucking tellys from the shop?

'Well your face will appear on every one of them TVs tonight when they switch on the news, unless we catch them first!'

Fortunately, Ricky was able to give a detailed description of the men involved and the van, along with part of the registration number, which was broadcast over the radio.

A short time later, Ricky heaved a huge sigh of relief when he was informed that the vehicle involved had been stopped at the city boundary. The TVs and electrical goods had been recovered, and the occupants had been apprehended.

It was now time for a relieved Ricky to head off home and 'Have a nice day!'

Zoo Time!

• • •

My old colleague and resident nightmare with the cult following, Donnie Henderson, called me the other day with this story.

'Harry boy! How the hell are you?' he asked.

'I'm fine, Donnie, just fine. How are you?' I replied politely.

'I'm not bad, Harry boy, but I'll tell you a wee story that just happened to me recently.

'I saw a job advertised in the police magazine for an odd-job man at the Edinburgh Zoo. So I called up for an interview and as luck would have it, I got the job.

'The first morning I started, I'm working with this auld grumpy zoo keeper, who handed me fish food and told me that the well stocked fish pond at the entrance was the first thing that the visitors saw when they entered the zoo, so it made a good impression on them if they saw all the fish up at the surface feeding and swimming about freely.

'I made my way down to the fish pond to feed them, only to discover them all floating upside down at the top – DEAD!

'I rushed up to tell the zoo keeper, who told me to get a net and a wheelbarrow, scoop all the dead fish up into the wheelbarrow and dump them over the wall into the lions' den.

'So I hurriedly did what I was told and rushed back to him and said, "What now?"'

'"Right!" he said. "The next big attraction for visitors as they enter the zoo is the chimpanzees swinging about from tree to tree, so nip down to the store and fill your wheelbarrow with apples and bananas and run over to the chimps' play area and give them it. That always brings them out for the visitors to see."

'So ah went over to the store, loaded up with fruit and headed for the chimpanzees' cage, but when I arrived, none of them was out. So I opened the door and went into the cage and found them all lying in their beds – DEAD!

'I rushed to tell the zoo keeper, who told me to load the wheelbarrow up with their dead bodies, run them up to the lions' area and throw them over the wall.

'So I hurriedly did as I was told and rushed back and said, "What now?"

'The zoo keeper said, "Right! A popular item that we sell in the shop is honey. So nip up to the back of the zoo to the bee hives, collect the honey and hand it into the shop for the girls to put into jars."

'Away I went, up to the back of the zoo to the bee hives, and when I got there . . .'

'Don't tell me! The bees were all dead!' I said, interrupting him.

'Exactly, Harry boy. You've guessed it. The bees were all dead. Some bugger had mashed them all up!

'I rushed back to tell the zoo keeper, who told me to get a brush, shovel and bucket, and to sweep up all the dead bees, fill the bucket and dump them over the wall into the lions' area.

'Once again, I hurriedly did as I was told and rushed back and said, "What now?"

'"I'll tell you what now! Now you can bugger off away

out the road, because I've got a couple of young lions getting delivered and I don't want you anywhere near them. You're nothing but bad luck!"

'So I buggered off and stood at the back of the wall of the lions' area, watching him as he was introducing these two young lions into the den and one of them came running up to the back wall. All of a sudden, I heard it asking a lioness, "What's it like in here, doll?"

'"Oh, it's very good!" she said. "We're well looked after in this zoo!"

'Then it asked her, "So! What's the grub like then?"

'And she replied, "Well, for our lunch, we just had fish and chimps wi' mushy bees!"'

There was silence for a moment before I put the phone down.

It's Who You Know
• • •

A female was stopped for speeding and while checking her driving licence the cop said, 'It states here that you should be wearing glasses!'

'I have contacts,' she replied.

To which the cop responded, 'I don't care who you know, missus, you're still getting a ticket!'

All Bets Off!

· · ·

A parent asked the local police officer for some help, informing him that his son had developed a gambling habit and he was anxious for him to grow out of it.

'I'll see what I can do to help you,' replied the police officer.

The policeman arranged for the boy to come to the station, so that he could speak with him regarding his gambling habit. After that his father called to collect him.

The boy was sent out of the room while the police officer spoke with the father.

'I think I've cured your son of his habit!' the officer said confidently. 'Let me explain how I did it.

As the father sat down at a desk opposite, the police officer said, 'While talking with your son about his habit, I noticed he was constantly staring at my moustache. Suddenly, in the middle of my lecture on gambling, he interrupted me and asked, "Constable Gray! Is that a real moustache, or is it a false one?"

'When I replied that it was a real one, he said, "I'll bet you a fiver it's a false one."

'I considered my position for a moment, then said, "All right, I'll take your bet. Now pull it and you'll see for yourself that it's a real moustache!"

'Of course, he lost the bet and I made him pay me the five pounds, as a lesson to him, but by doing so, I believe I've cured him of his gambling habit!' he said, pleased with the result of the action he had taken.

'Oh no!' groaned the father. 'A fiver? The wee bugger bet me a tenner that he would pull your moustache during your talk with him!'

Horse's Arse
• • •

Two traffic cops pull over a driver for speeding.

After informing the driver why he was stopped, one of the cops starts to write out the speeding ticket, but is continually distracted by a fly that's circling around his head.

'Damn fly. It's a bloody nuisance!' he says.

'Circle fly,' the driver remarks.

'What did you say?' the cop asks.

'I said it's a circle fly!' the driver repeats.

'A circle fly? I've never heard of that before. How do you know that?' he enquires.

'Because I have stables and they're usually found circling around a horse's arse! That's why.'

The cop is furious with this remark and says to the driver, 'Are you insinuating that I'm a horse's arse?'

To which the driver replies, 'Certainly not, Officer! But you'll have a hard job trying to convince that fly!'

Fact or Fiction?

• • •

The brief scenario is as follows:

Johnny takes apart a leftover firework from Guy Fawkes Night and empties the contents into a small bottle, attaches a wick and blows up an ant-hill in the garden.

In the 1960s, the ant-hill would be destroyed along with the ants. Nothing more said.

Present day, the police would be contacted, who in turn would notify MI6 and the Bomb Squad.

As a result of their inquiry, Johnny would be charged with perpetrating acts of terrorism.

His parents and close relatives would be investigated and removed from their family homes.

All computers and mobile telephones would be confiscated for examination of their records and Johnny's father's name would be added to a terror watch list and never allowed to holiday abroad again!

Fact or fiction?

It Never Ends

• • •

A convict escaped from prison and returned to his house where he knocked on the door.

His wife answered the door to him and said, 'Where the hell have you been?

'According to Sky News, you escaped from prison six hours ago!'

That's My Dad

...

I was writing a wee story about my late father the other day and by, pure accident, I came across some interesting facts that I was unaware of, so let me tell you them first.

At the age of thirteen, having left school, he worked as a motorbike dispatch rider for the Fire Brigade and by sixteen, two years into World War Two, he wanted to serve his country and so enrolled in the Royal Navy.

Due to being very tall for his age, he easily passed for eighteen years old and was accepted, no questions asked.

Several convoys later, at the end of the war, he was accepted into the fire brigade full-time, having failed the medical for the police, because he had flat feet!

Accepted by the fire brigade, he was to become the youngest fireman in Britain and had the distinction of having served his country and been awarded six medals as a result. Something that a lot of his colleagues in the brigade hadn't done!

He also continued to serve in the armed forces, by enlisting in the Royal Navy Volunteer Reserves, and when he was required to resign years later, due to a back injury he'd sustained, he found it hard to accept, so he immediately contacted the Royal Engineers Territorial Army Reserves and enlisted with them, serving for a further twelve years.

He was also very much a royalist during this time and would never tolerate anyone talking badly about any part of the Armed Forces, and I mean to the extent where he would have no hesitation in resorting to physical assault!

With this in mind, I will now relate an incident that took place one evening in a pub in Glasgow, while he and I were sitting having a quiet drink, awaiting the arrival of one of his ex-army buddies.

We had been sitting at a table in the middle of the lounge for about half an hour, when in walked his old mate Cameron.

During the ensuing conversation, Cameron intimated that he had arranged with his daughter's boyfriend, a newspaper reporter, to join us for a drink.

In the interim period, before he arrived, they were talking about the latest news regarding two young army squaddies who had been killed whilst on duty, and how tragic it had been, when the door of the pub opened and in came Cameron's friend the reporter.

He joined us at the table and after the polite introductions I went to the bar to fetch some drinks.

On my return to the table, they were discussing the situation regarding the young soldiers, and the reporter said that he was doing an article on them and that's why he'd been late in arriving.

My father then remarked that it was sad to hear about the loss of life of two young soldiers who were the pawns, placed in a situation they would rather not have been in.

The reporter replied flippantly, 'They get well paid to be there, so they know what they're doing when they join up, and dying for their country is part of the game!'

The situation was becoming very heated within a very short space of time and I immediately feared for the smug reporter's boyish good looks, for I could see the hackles beginning to rise in my father's neck as he pointed out that 'they were only young boys, sent over to another country to save lives by keeping both sides apart and thereby maintaining peace.'

The reporter was having none of it and replied with a short, sharp and resounding, 'Tough!'

The word 'Tough' had barely left his lips, and I doubt very much if he saw it coming, or remembers much about it afterwards, but it coincided with my father's big fist coming the opposite way, directly across the table and connecting full on with the reporter's face, knocking him clean off his seat, where he landed flat out on his back, about ten feet away, totally unconscious!

Cameron did not appear to be the least bit surprised at the outcome of the heated discussion between my father and his daughter's boyfriend and he signalled for me to get my father out of the pub quickly, while he attempted to try and bring the boy round.

Along with my father, we left the premises and stopped a taxi to take us home, although I did encounter some resistance from my father, who wanted to remain there and finish off his drink.

About an hour after we had arrived back at his house, the phone rang and I answered it. It was Cameron.

I made to apologise for my father's behaviour towards his friend, but Cameron interrupted.

'Are ye kidding? Fuck him! I knew he couldn't keep his big mouth shut. That's why I invited him to come along. He was bound to say something during the night about the army or the navy, and knowing your old man, it was only a matter of time, but I didn't expect the big man to react so quickly. What a dull yin he gave him. He's been totally sparkled ever since!'

On hearing this, I had to ask Cameron, 'So why invite him along if you knew that he would say something that would upset my dad and end up like it did?'

'Cause I can't stand him, but I couldn't do anything myself! He's been dating my daughter, but he's bad news – pardon the pun. He's a cheeky, arrogant bastard and I don't like him one bit. But my daughter doesn't see it and refuses to listen to me.

'Listen, Harry, I've been in your old man's company long enough to know how he reacts to anybody making remarks about the forces, and I also knew this bastard wouldn't be able to bite his tongue once they started talking. He's a reporter after all, can't keep his big mouth shut, but he'll maybe shut it now!

'By the way! He didn't remember a bloody thing about what happened tonight!' Cameron paused before adding, 'He's some man, big Freddie, you don't mess about with him.'

So, in effect, he had orchestrated the entire event, knowing my father would not be able to sit and listen to someone bad-mouthing the armed forces without reacting.

However, I'm glad to report that it backfired on Cameron when his daughter announced she was pregnant, and it didn't need to be front-page news to guess who the father was.

Now he had a future son-in-law who couldn't keep his mouth shut, and a pregnant daughter who couldn't keep her legs shut!

Restoring Life
...

A cop was driving along a country road one day when a hare ran across the road in front of him.

He quickly took evasive action and slammed on the brakes and swerved, but could not avoid accidentally hitting the hare.

He got out of his police vehicle to see if it was alright, but unfortunately the hare was dead.

As he stood at the side of the road holding it, a car with a lady driver pulled up to see what was wrong.

The police officer told her what had happened.

'Hold on a minute. I have an idea,' said the lady, as she produced a small can from her handbag and sprayed the hare.

Suddenly the hare started to move and, as the policeman put it down, it waved its little paw at them and hopped off down the road, stopping every few feet to turn back and wave to them while they looked on. It continued doing this until it was out of sight. The policeman was amazed by this and asked the lady what was in the can.

The lady replied, 'Hairspray! Restores life to your dead hair and gives it a permanent wave!'

The Body Swerve

...

On certain occasions when they were short of manpower, you would be detailed an area to patrol, outwith your normal beat area. Such was the case one nightshift when Dick was sent to Dalkeith to work.

As luck would have it, the duty sergeant was an old buddy of his from the CID who had been recently promoted.

As a result, he was detailed to take out the divisional Land Rover and patrol the outlying areas that had shops and factories.

The area was huge, stretching some 400 square miles in total, and was policed during the day by single-man-operated stations, but at night it was patrolled by the divisional HQ.

By three a.m. he had covered the southern part of the beat area and was now heading up to the northern part, near to the city boundary, an area that he was familiar with and had worked on several occasions. He stopped next to a small line of shops for a short break and a rest from driving in the constant rain.

After a short while, he drove along to the local bowling club to check it, and as he was walking along the path, he stumbled and fell over something in the dark.

Getting up from the ground, he put on his torch to discover he had tripped over the dead body of a well known alcoholic from the area.

It appeared that he had fallen over whilst under the influence and had choked to death on his own vomit.

By this point, it was getting close to finishing time and he did not wish to incur overtime filling out a sudden-death report and a lengthy visit to the mortuary. So he lifted the deceased up and placed him in the rear of the police vehicle and drove him over the boundary, into another force area, where he stopped the vehicle, dragged him out, propped him up against a newsagent's shop doorway, and left him to be discovered.

This accomplished, he then made his way back to the police station to go off duty as normal.

However, on reporting for duty the following evening, he was taken aside by the shift sergeant and informed about the local alcoholic, from their area, who had died from choking on his own vomit, and had been discovered by the early shift of the adjoining force, in the doorway of the newsagent's.

He then asked him if he knew anything about it.

Dick calmly asked the sergeant why he was telling him all this, when the deceased was found by another force, and in another area!

To which the sergeant responded by saying that he found it difficult to understand how his body should be discovered three miles away in another force area, having been informed by the staff at the bowling club that he was so drunk he couldn't walk and, as a result, they had sat him down outside on one of the benches at the club, prior to locking up for the night!

'Now! How do you figure he managed to get to where he was found, when he couldn't walk the length of himself, because he was that drunk?'

Dick paused for a moment, thinking about an answer, then smiled at the newly promoted sergeant and said, 'Conundrums were never my strong point, Sergeant, but you were in the CID long enough to work it out for yourself!'

Then as he opened the office door to leave, he added, 'I would have thought it was dead obvious to you sergeant . . . he drove there!'

Stress
· · ·

The other day I called at the police doctor's surgery and told him I was suffering from stress and I was losing my temper with my colleagues and insulting them.

'You've got to help me, Doctor!' I said.

The police doctor looked at me and said, 'Okay, Morris, tell me about your problem.'

To which I answered, 'I just did, you stupid old bugger!'

The Story

· · ·

Wee Davie boy, as he was affectionately known around the place, was a local lad from the Drumchapel scheme in Glasgow, and worked with his father on a farm, tending a flock of sheep.

He was the youngest of eight sons born to big Jesse, a loving family man who stayed up a close of a newly built council house tenement in a brand-new housing scheme that had recently sprung up in the west end of Glasgow.

Wee Willie Donnelly, the local elected councillor for 'the Drum', was waging war with the gang from the nearby Clydebank area, who were known as the Philobeans.

One morning, the good people of the Drum awoke to discover a big team of the Philobeans loitering with intent at the bottom of Achamore Hill, blocking the main gateway to the scheme.

On being informed of their presence in the area, Willie quickly raised the alarm and summoned up a gathering of his finest troops, to rally round and congregate at the top of the hill in order to defend the Drum!

Within minutes, the entire male population of the Drum, referred to as the Lastrites, appeared out from the scheme's four most popular Bs: the Bookies, the Bingo, the Boozers and the Brothels, the latter affectionately renamed by Willie during his election campaign as your everyday, family-friendly sauna and massage parlour.

They all stood about, tensely psyching each other out while waiting anxiously for the slightest movement or signal that would be the beginning of the physical engagement, commonly referred to as a 'stooshie'. Now they were gathering telephone votes for being the latest reality TV show to be fronted by Simon Cowell and his Syco TV company and called *The X-Rated Strictly Come Chibbing*.

The odd mobile phone would interrupt the tense, eerie silence, with a chart-topping ring tone, providing the receiver with a well-rehearsed excuse in order to avoid any confrontation, or physical injury being endured by one's ever so fragile 'Jean Brodie'.

Such excuses were to become common knowledge amongst the most notable of shite bags, who boasted to being lifelong members of the Lastrites.

For example, excuses such as:

'Eh, Willie! I'll need tae go. Ah forgot that oor Maisie works tae five o'clock on a Friday and I've got tae collect the weans fae the school!'

'Christ! Would ye look at the time? If ah don't appear at the hoose very shortly with a Big Mac and French fries for her indoors, she'll withdraw my conjugal rights for a month!'

And the most popular excuse and common complaint of all:

'You'll have to excuse me, Willie, but I believe my bomb doors are starting to open and shut by themselves and I'm about to partake in an uncontrolled bowel movement, whereby I am likely to part company with my entire insides, culminating in my designer Calvin Klein 'Cary Grants' being leggered with one's own excrement!'

'What?' a confused Willie would enquire, seeking a forthcoming, simple explanation.

'I'm about to shite myself, wee man!'

It was during all this negative activity surrounding him that Willie also received an unexpected telephone call. This was no ordinary pre-planned excuse by him, for this call came from the fearsome Gareth, the tallest, strongest and meanest dude in the entire Philobean gang.

On Wee Willie answering his mobile phone, Gareth immediately greeted him with the following:

'Who's that?'

'Well considering it was you that called me, ya diddy, there has got tae be a significant clue in there for ye!' Willie sarcastically answered.

There was a pause for a few moments, while Gareth, whom we now know had a reputation for being big and strong, and now had the distinction of adding the words 'totally thick' at the end of his CV, as he digested Willie's response.

'Is that Wee Willie Donnelly?' he enquired.

'Correct!' Willie replied. 'And you, my friend, must be the guy from TV's *Mastermind*, so can I pass on to your next question, 'cause I'm really a wee bit busy at the moment, Magnus.'

This was followed by another few moments of muffled pausing, coupled with some loud grunting and growling noises..

'D-D-Do you know who I am?' asked the irate Gareth in his deep, gravelly voice that can only be attained from years of swallowing large whiskies, followed by the whisky glass!

Now at this particular point, Willie is not one hundred

per cent focussed on the person on the other end of his mobile, and to be fair to him, his mind is fully occupied with the more urgent matter at hand, but he can't resist responding to the caller's question.

'No! I don't know who you are, but let me try and work it out for your sake and my sanity.

'Now, you've just called me on my mobile phone, so ye know my number, but ye don't know who I am. But then, ye don't know who you are either, so I suppose you've got tae be one of two persons.

'Ye're either Tommy Sheridan, looking tae book a sauna and massage, followed by half an hour on the sunbed, or ye're that pussy impersonator George Galloway, collecting for Cash for Kids.

'So reveal yourself, caller: who the fuck are you?'

An angry, frustrated voice stammered out loudly over his mobile phone, in instalments.

'I'm GA-GA-GA-RETH!' he blurted out aggressively.

Quick as a flash, Willie responded to his stuttering reply.

'GA-GA-GA-RETH! Whit, GATES? It's a bad time tae call me up, son, especially if ye're after a booking at the Community Centre. I've already got Will Young, but can ye maybe call me back later in the week? I'm looking for somebody for Burns' Night at the Miners' Welfare!'

After the dust settled and Gareth finally managed to identify himself as the real deal, he proceeded to offer Willie a 'Get Out of Jail Free' solution to the present dilemma he now faced, with a straightforward proposition.

Why should they all have to fight, when he, GA-GA-GA-RETH, was prepared to offer a square-go to anyone of Willie's Lastrites with a death wish and daft enough to fight him, with a 'Winner Takes All' bet!

The stake would be, if Gareth beat up Willie's challenger, and presented him with the Lastrites' head on the end of his chib, then Willie and the Lastrites would have to serve the Philobeans forever.

But – and it was a very big BUT!

If by some miracle the challenger chosen by the Lastrites to represent them in the fight was fortunate enough to beat the mighty and invincible Gareth, then the Philobeans would have to serve them, and be ruled over by Councillor Donnelly.

That simple!

However, for what it is worth, there wasn't a hope in hell of that happening, according to the latest betting odds from William Hill the bookmaker.

Willie thought for a moment before readily accepting the challenge and stated the immortal words, 'Ye're on, big man!'

At that, Willie hung up the phone to focus his attention on choosing his champion challenger, among the many Lastrite candidates assembled before him, and also to see if there was anyone stupid enough to volunteer to fight Gareth.

As he perused the faces of his gang members, he immediately saw the answer to his prayers and the solution to the Lastrites' problem – a potential home banker and odds-on bet: in none other than JIMMY THE BLADE!

Jimmy the Blade was the eldest son of a former Glasgow time-served 'Razor King' from the Gorbals, who according to his own CV had administered more 'extreme makeover face lifts' than California's very own renowned plastic surgeon, Doctor Garth Fisher!

'Right, Jimmy the Blade! I'm going to bestow the honour on you. What about it?

'How would you like to represent your fellow Lastrites and take this big ugly bastert out?

'And when I say take him out, ah don't mean tae the pictures! Ah mean tae say, Jimmy, you tick all the boxes for being a mean bastert yerself, and I don't think I need to remind you that it was only last week ye were charged with three serious assaults and banged up in the Bar L on remand.

'Ye must still be champing at the bit tae chib some other bugger?'

Jimmy looked at Willie, taking in every word of his somewhat accurate description of him, before replying.

'Listen, don't get me wrang, Willie, ah'd love tae chib him, but see they three serious-assault charges, they were for slapping the wean, her mammy and her granny. They dropped the charges after a few days. Ah jist exaggerated the incident a wee bit tae look good in front of the boys in the Stab Inn, so that I could get a few beers on the house,' Jimmy responded rather sheepishly, and was now standing there, resembling a rather more subdued and sedate Jimmy the 'Blunt' Blade!

Staring at refusal in his first attempt to recruit a suitable challenger to face Gareth, Willie turned his attention to his second in command, 'Mad Dog Magoorie'.

In his last skirmish, it was reported that he had bitten off his opponent's ear, quickly followed by part of his nose, and was in the process of going all out for the full set of Ear, Nose and Throat when his opponent managed to get his hand up in time to stop him, resulting in Mad Dog biting off two of his fingers and swallowing them.

'Mad Dog! How about it? What about adding to your gruesome reputation by taking a bite oot o' the big man's balls?'

Mad Dog gave Willie one of his sinister, growling stares before looking down at his watch and saying in a surprisingly soft whimper, 'Bloody hell! Is that the right time? Ah better get my arse up that road afore I'm in big trouble wi' the wife. She's got me babysitting tonight, so that her and the daughter can go tae the bingo. Ah'm sure a mentioned it tae ye earlier, Willie, It's the big Snowball link-up prize tonight, see ye!'

At that, Mad Dog scurried away with his tail between his legs.

As Willie watched him go, he whispered under his breath, 'I knew it – never trust a dog, or a man that can lick his own balls.'

With two down, it had to be third time lucky, thought Willie, crossing his fingers, toes and eyes!

Step forward, 'Billy the Blacksmith'.

'You've got more brands to your name than there are in the entire ASDA superstore. How about branding this big diddy and stick a roasting hot poker right up his kilt in true Burns tradition?

'After all, I was responsible for pushing through your

housing grant so you could get help tae re-tile your barn roof and double-glaze your windows!'

Billy stared at Willie with a lack of expression on his face, as if appearing to think over what Willie has just asked him to do, and then he spoke.

'Willie, I would be honoured! And I would do it in a minute.' Then he paused before continuing. 'But I'm waiting for the engineer coming fae Sky to erect my new satellite dish so that I can watch the last episode of *The Simpsons* after. It's the one where Homer thinks he's dying, but he's really just dreaming. Dae ye know the one ah'm talking about?'

Willie's chin hit the floor as, one by one, excuse after excuse, they all slinked away, leaving two Lastrites, namely Davie boy, who had only turned up to deliver some milk and cheese for the troops, along with his wee pal Brian the baker, who brought along some fresh bread rolls.

Willie surveyed the scene, and looking at the two of them standing there, he announced, 'Right, you two better sort it out between you, who's getting chibbed wi' the big man over there. And don't be worrying about the outcome, the Council will fund all your funeral arrangements, and I'll personally notify your parents and let them know whit happened and that you went down fighting bravely to the bitter end. No doubt the *Daily Record* will also do a front-page spread on ye, so good luck.'

At that, Willie rushed to leave, but Brian was having none of it.

'Ho! Where exactly dae ye think you're going, Willie?'

Willie called back that he had an important Council

meeting to attend, which could effectively change their entire way of life in Drumchapel.

'Is that right, Willie?' Davie boy replied. 'Well the wee man here has also got an important meeting wi' yon big man over the road that could effectively and seriously change his entire life, never mind his entire face intae the bargain!'

'Correct, Davie boy. Well said,' responded Brian, who then paused for a moment, thinking over what Davie boy had just said, then the penny dropped.

'Wait a cotton-picking minute there. Why me? How come I have a meeting wi' the big man and no' you?'

'Because I'm much younger and have my whole life in front of me,' Davie replied.

'What? And I don't, like?' Brian asked. 'Ah mean tae say, mine isn't exactly behind me. Mine is in front of me as well.'

'Well no' for much longer,' Davie said. 'No' after the big man has chibbed ye a few times, ye don't. So here's my plan. Ye play deid after the initial few and he might no' be too bothered about continuing tae stab ye!'

Brian isn't paying too much attention to Davie boy, and is still trying to work out the age difference between them.

'No! No! No! Davie, there's only two years of a difference between us, so that's no' fair . . . Let's just toss a coin, or cut cards tae decide who gets done in!'

'Sorry, Brian, but I don't know how tae play cards – too young!'

'Well ye better learn fast, 'cause I don't know how tae

die, and ah cannae fight either, but somebody – as in you or me – is heading for a big Wilkinson sword being deposited up one's arse.'

They both sat down in total silence for a moment, making weird faces and rubbing their heads, while they pondered what to do.

'Ah know!' Brian said. 'We challenge him tae a pie-making competition. I'll beat him hands down.'

Davie boy shakes his head.

'He wants tae be involved in a fight, no' *Ready Steady Cook*!'

They both settled down again and Brian said, 'I've got it. Paper, Stone and Scissors!'

'Paper, Stone and Scissors?' Davie replied. 'Whit, are we gonnae hit him wi' them and see whit one gets him really mad?'

'Don't be daft, it's a game. Stone blunts scissors, scissors cut the paper, and the paper . . .' Davie paused before continuing, 'Stuff it! You're right, let's just toss a coin.'

Davie produced a coin from his pocket and handed it to Brian, who flipped it up in the air and said, 'Heads ah win, tails you lose, awright?'

'Awright!'

The coin landed on the floor and they both rushed over to check it out. Brian was delighted.

'Tails it is. Ya beauty! You lose, Davie boy, no hard feelings.'

'Hold on a minute. Let's make it best out of three.'

Brian stared at Davie for a moment, before reluctantly agreeing to his request.

'Awright! Since you're my best pal, we'll make it best out of three. Same rules.'

Brian took hold of the coin, flipped it into the air and repeated his saying.

'Heads ah win, tails you lose.'

As the coin landed on the floor for the second time, they both rushed over to check it.

Brian immediately started dancing ecstatically, punching the air.

'Yes! Yes! Yes! Heads ah win! Go for it, Davie boy, he's all yours. Here, let me help you on with your hoodie.'

Davie has his head down.

'That's no' fair. Ah think you cheated me! Let me see that coin.'

Brian showed him both sides of the coin.

'See! Head on this side and a tail on this side. Now don't be a bad loser, you've lost fair and square. But then again, Davie boy, if you look at what is on offer as a reward for setting about the big man, you've actually won, and I'm the loser!'

Davie gave him a look of confusion.

'I've won? I have won? How the fuck did ye work that one out?' Davie then paused for a moment, realising what Brian just said. 'Reward! What reward?'

'Only the best council house in the whole of Drumchapel, rent free for the rest of your short life, a food hamper, compliments of Marks and Spencer, wi' a personal greeting fae the bird that talks on the advert, and last but not least, the icing on the cake, the star prize is . . . Wait for it!'

'Aw, hurry up, Brian, the excitement is running down my legs.'

'Okay! The star prize is a weekend away tae the Dutch House Caravan Park in Prestwick, wi' . . . Jordan!'

'Jordan? Big tits, page-three Jordan? Are ye joking?'

'Aye! It's Madonna!' said Brian nonchalantly.

'Madonna? Singer, songwriter Madonna, married tae Mabawsa Ritchie that makes the films?'

'It's Guy!'

'Well I know it's a guy . . . But that Madonna?'

'Eh . . . No exactly that Madonna! It's Willie Donnelly's eldest daughter Madonna! So, what about that then?'

Davie quietly ran it over in his mind.

'Is Willie's eldest daughter no' called Bonnie?'

'That was just a nickname the boys gave to her on the fifth of November last year, because every guy at the firework display had been on top of her.

'Anyways, she's mad keen tae reward the winner wi' a dirty weekend! Purely as a prize for being brave and absolutely nothing to do with the fact that she's turned out to be a raving nympho like her mammy!'

Davie mulled it over in his mind and rubbed his chin.

'A weekend away wi' big Madonna. That is awesome, man!'

'No! She's awesome, but in saying that, she's built for comfort. So it's settled then, you're doing it?'

'It's settled. I'm doing it!'

As they both shook hands on the decision, Brian said, 'Right! I'll leave ye tae have a few minutes tae yerself and make peace wi' yer maker, while I go out and get you a selection of good chibs and your body bag!'

'My body bag? Did you just say my body bag?'

'Don't be daft. Ah said your body vest! As in your favourite Tartan Army top, personally autographed by Sir Furious. Ye know, you're a dead ringer for Mel Gibson in it!'

'Dae ye think so?' Davie asked.

'No' really, but at this moment in time, it's nice tae be nice, and any old excuse goes down well!' replied Brian.

During all this time, Ga-Ga-Ga-reth had been marching up and down in the hot midday sun, kitted out in all the latest sports gear from the Littlewoods catalogue, as modeled by Trinny and Susannah. He was spouting all kinds of threats of abuse in order for them to hurry up and decide who was coming out to face him and get chibbed in the process.

Time was getting on and he wanted to have it over and done with quickly, so that he could be back home with his feet up before the start of the new series of *CSI Miami* started on Channel Five.

In the meantime, Brian was cleaning Davie's new Nike trainers and ironing his Umbro joggies, in order to make him look presentable for his parents when they were summoned to the city mortuary to identify his body.

Davie was kneeling down and making peace with the Lord. As he did so, he picked up a large prayer book, lying on a table in the Lastrites' makeshift HQ tent, and began to read passages from it, slowly turning the pages, desperately seeking some kind of inspiration.

He spoke loudly the words of his prayer:

'Lord! Ah'd just like tae say I'm sorry for using the occasional swear word, sometimes ah just cannae help myself.

'Oh, and that incident the other night, when that sheep was looking over the edge o' the hill, ah hold my hands up! Ah was genuinely taking a piss and when I looked over and saw it, I thought it was going tae jump, or I would never have rushed over tae rescue it.

'And it was also a total surprise tae me, and a pure coincidence, that I just happened tae be standing right behind it when it decided tae back itself up and onto me, ah swear!

'Crikey! There I go again, swearing!

'But ah just wanted ye tae know that it was a genuine accident, and I certainly don't make a habit of it, and even if I did, ah definitely wouldn't have picked a ram for my first conquest, that's for sure.'

He then paused for a moment, deep in thought.

'Oh, and another thing, Lord. If I get through this square-go wi' Gareth, and I'm still in one piece, can ye have a wee look at rewarding me as well, 'cause I think when I was getting circumcised, the Rabbi, bless him, didn't have his proper reading glasses with him, and as a result, he cut off a bit more than he should have, and now I'm lagging a good two tae three inches behind my brothers Eli and Abie.

'Ah know they say size isn't everything, but them that say it are just a bunch o' lying basterts, who you'll find are all well endowed wi' more than their fair share and don't want any extra competition!

'Lord, you've helped me before, when ye gave me the strength I needed to see off that big lion that attacked the flock and tried tae kill some o' the sheep. Ah managed tae fight it off and save them . . .

'And there was the other time, when yon big bear came calling and grabbed a ewe. Ah wrestled wi' it and managed tae get it tae release its grip . . .

'Ah know ye were there wi' me, giving me your support to carry out these deeds, but, Lord, this is totally different here.

'This big evil bastert is pure mental and has got a heart o' a lion and the height, weight and strength of a grizzly bear. Oh, and did I mention that he was a complete and utter maniac, who gives me nightmares just thinking about him? You don't know whit he's capable of.'

Davie paused for a moment to compose himself.

'Look! I'll tell ye what, Lord.

'First and foremost, see if ye could maybe help me out again this time wi' a wee bit o' handers, like striking him down wi' a massive heart attack, or maybe even a severe stroke down the one side, just enough tae paralyse him, so that he qualifies for disability benefits. It would be very much appreciated, and wi' regards tae my other requests . . .

'Ah would settle for a penis pump!'

Davie was interrupted by the return of an excited Brian.

'Check out this lot, Davie boy. I've only went and got you the latest in stab vests, and a sponsorship deal for the day wi' Adidas! Oh, and sign yer name at the bottom o' this piece o' paper.'

That said, he handed Davie a pen.

'What is this for?' Davie asked.

'It's just a form tae say that I'm your next of kin!'

'Piss off, Brian. I don't need any of this.'

'Excuse me, Davie boy, but believe me, ye frigging do. I've just seen the big man over there at his press conference, and he's well tooled up and itching tae get started.

'He's got more steak knives in his waist band than Galloway the butchers! So believe me, son, ye need it! So sign there.'

He then paused for a moment, before adding, 'Mind you, instead of asking for forgiveness, you could have asked the Lord for the return of Frankie Vaughan, with the suggestion of another knife amnesty in Glasgow!'

Brian lifted up the stab vest.

'Here, let me help you with this. It'll protect ye a wee bit.'

Davie shrugged him away and said, 'There's no need, Brian. The Lord is going to protect me, and has provided for me.'

'Look, Davie boy, I admire your faith, but I have two words for you to consider: "Jesus" and a very big "Cross"!'

'I have complete faith in the Lord,' Davie stoutly replied.

'Can I just remind you: so did his only son.'

There was silence as Brian stepped back and looked at Davie.

'Were you smoking that wacky baccy while I was away?'

'Don't be daft . . . Nae matches!'

Brian sat down, produced a bottle of Buckfast wine from his pocket and poured out a glass. On seeing it, Davie backed off.

'And don't pour me any of that, either. Ah don't need it.'

'That's not for you. It's for me; ah need it. Ah'm running about there like a blue-arsed fly, trying tae dae some last-minute deals for us wi' Max Clifford, *Hello!* and Anderson Maguire!'

'Anderson Maguire. Who's that?' Davie asked.

'Some funeral parlour where the family come first. Except in your case!' Brian replied.

'Well, ye can cancel that one, 'cause this isn't happening!'

They both paused for a moment to reconsider. Brian said, 'So is this all the thanks I get from a mate who's about to depart this world? Ah just don't understand you, Davie boy!'

'Ye don't understand me, Brian, 'cause ye don't listen. I've told you, the Lord has shown me the way; he will protect me and he has provided for me.'

All the time, Davie was holding on tightly to his prayer book.

'With what, Davie boy, the words in a book? So you're gonnae walk right up tae him and read him a story? Ah can just see it now!

'Excuse me a minute, Gareth, but before ye separate my head from my body, can I maybe read you a chapter from the new Harry Potter book?

'That will really hit him hard. The poor bugger will be trembling in his Jesus sandals.

'Look, Davie! Let me phone over tae Glesca Airport and recruit John Smeaton and a few of the baggage handlers tae come over and give ye handers!'

Davie boy shook his head and looked at Brian condescendingly.

'No, Brian! I've told you repeatedly. The Lord has given me the necessary tool to beat Gareth. He'll not be getting close enough for me tae read him anything . . .'

'Awright, Davie boy! So is this the part in the story where ye suddenly produce your slingshot and stone?'

At that, Davie put his hand into the prayer book and produced a very large pistol from inside the book covers. He waved it in front of Brian and said, 'No, Brian! This is the part in the story where I suddenly produce the most powerful handgun in the world, as in this big bloody 44 Magnum that some fly bugger was hiding in the good book.'

Hasta la vista . . . Baby!

The R.U.C. love their Guinness
While the Metropolitan love a tot
But we're the Glesca Polis Force
And we drink the bloody lot!!!

Harry Says, 'Share With Me!'

• • •

Former police officer Harry Morris, author of the popular *Harry the Polis* series of books, is planning to publish book number seven of his funny short polis stories:

Harry the Polis, Up Tae My Neck In Paperwork!

He would like to extend an invitation to all serving and retired polis, along with all FSO staff, to contribute a story to future publications and allow the popular, hilarious series to continue.

Stories must be of a humorous nature and can even be a short scenario of an incident that you would like the author to expand upon. (All names will be changed to protect the guilty.)

We are all very much aware of the seriousness and important side of the job, when serving the public. That's why the humour we enjoy in our duties is a very important feature to our work.

So why not share it with your colleagues and the public by giving everyone a laugh, as opposed to reading about horrific day-to-day crimes that we see daily in the press that are forced upon us.

Just send stories, poems, anecdotes, jokes or tales to: harry@harrythepolis.com
or visit the website at www.harrythepolis.com

The author will be sure to credit you with your submission. However, if you wish to remain anonymous, this will also be respected by the author. The main objective is not to make fun of the police force, but to write about the humour we all enjoy and contribute to within it.

So why don't you start writing and let me hear from you? We all have a funny story we have been involved with, why not share it?

Thank you

· · ·

I hope you enjoyed reading this book of stories in the *Harry the Polis* series as much as I enjoyed writing it.

To all my former colleagues, past, present and future police officers, I would say: if you can't laugh at yourselves, then leave the job to others.

Acknowledgements

• • •

The author would like to thank Ian Taylor, John Thompson, Alan Ritchie, Ian Whitelaw, Tom Kelly, Bill Hunter, Dick Waddell, Jack Hunter, Tom McNulty and David Marr for their contributions. I hope I did them justice.

Website: www.harrythepolis.com
Email: harry@harrythepolis.com

Harry Morris aka Harry the Polis, is available for Stand-Up Comedy Storytelling, Guest Speaking, Script/Sketch Writing.

All enquiries to info@harrythepolis.com

Postal address:

P.O. Box 7031
Glasgow
G44 3YN

Harry Morris is registered with the Scottish Book Trust for Live Literature events